Knowing God's Truth Workbook

KNOWING GOD'S TRUTH WORKBOOK

An Introduction to
Systematic Theology

JON NIELSON

CROSSWAY®

WHEATON, ILLINOIS

Crossway is a publishing ministry of Good News Publishers.

NP		33	32	31	30	29	28	27	26	25	24	23
14	13	12	11	10	9	8	7	6	5	4	3	2	1

CONTENTS

INTRODUCTION

Welcome to this introductory study of systematic theology—*Knowing God's Truth*!

This workbook is designed to be used as a supplementary resource in conjunction with your reading of the full book. There are summaries of the chapters in *Knowing God's Truth*, but also questions for you to answer that will help you dive deeper into the material—and make sure you're grasping all of it. Ideally, you should read the chapters in the book first, then move through the workbook chapters to reinforce and capture all you're learning.

You can use this on your own or in the context of a small group, Sunday school class, or Bible class in a school setting. You'll benefit greatly from discussion with other Christians as you learn this material.

So dive in and see what God has to teach you about himself in his wonderful word!

WHAT IS THEOLOGY?

The word *theology* literally means "God talk." The root *theo* means "God," and the suffix, *-logy*, comes from the Greek word *logos*, which means "word." So when we do theology, we are talking together about God and things that relate to God. Theology, broadly, is the study of God. When you think about it this way, hopefully the term seems less intimidating or alienating. After all, we already do this when we study God's word; we study God.

In "systematic theology," we are simply bringing organization to our theological thinking by using some categories for the way we think and talk about God, sin, human beings, salvation, and so on. It's a bit like organizing the different parts of the wardrobe in your closet: pants, shirts, socks, underwear—you get the picture. In *Knowing God's Truth* and this workbook, we're going to organize the "closet" of our theology into distinct sections, trying to pull together the Bible's teaching on specific subjects and topics.

Respond to the following questions as you begin to dive into the study of theology through this book and workbook:

1. What about systematic theology sounds intimidating to you? Does it sound exciting, boring, overly academic, or something else? Explain.

2. Why is it helpful to be reminded that everyone is a theologian of some sort (even the atheist who says, "There is no god!")? If we're all theologians already, why should we put time and effort into working through our theological beliefs?

3. Jot down a few of your biggest and most confusing theological questions. What have you wrestled with—about God, salvation, sin, and so on—recently in your walk with God?

WHY DOES THEOLOGY MATTER?

Review pages 3–5 in *Knowing God's Truth*

One of the common objections from Christians today, when it comes to studying theology, is that it's too academic or "heady." "Just love Jesus and others," some say. "Why spend time getting into the weeds of theology? Let's keep things simple!" The simple response to this idea is that God gave us the Bible—his inspired word—which tells us marvelous things about him. To care about theology is actually to care about God himself. As we learn theology, we also find that it is deeply practical; what we believe about God, our world, and ourselves has very real implications for the decisions we make every day.

1. What objections have you heard in your social circles to studying theology? What misunderstandings about the Christian life do some of those objections reveal?

2. How might we see the study of theology as a demonstration of our love for God himself?

3. Why does what we believe have practical implications for how we live?

BIBLICAL, HISTORICAL, AND SYSTEMATIC THEOLOGY

Review pages 5–7 in *Knowing God's Truth*

It's important to understand the different *kinds* of theology that a person can study. "Biblical theology" involves tracing themes and ideas throughout the Bible as they are progressively revealed. "Historical theology" is more tied to developments in theological thinking through the centuries; it explores how theological beliefs and formulations came about in and through the church over time. "Systematic theology"—what we're doing—certainly takes biblical and historical theology into account, but it is more focused on organizing theological thought into specific categories or topics, summarizing the Bible's teaching on each particular idea.

1. What might be some benefits of learning to do biblical theology well? Why is it important to understand how a theme or idea develops throughout the Bible?

2. How can historical theology be a valuable field of study? What can be helpful about getting perspectives from Christians in different centuries, countries, or cultures?

3. In what ways have you already done some systematic theology—even in small and simple ways? What biblical themes or ideas have you tried to summarize for yourself?

DOCTRINE OF SCRIPTURE AND DOCTRINE OF GOD

Review pages 8–9 in *Knowing God's Truth*

The first two big categories of systematic theology in this study are the doctrine of *Scripture* and the doctrine of *God* (sometimes called theology proper). When we study the doctrine of Scripture, we're trying to answer questions about the Bible: What *is* the Bible? What do we mean when we talk about the Bible being "inspired" or "infallible"? How is the Bible different from other religious books? When we study the doctrine of God, we're focusing on God himself: What is he like (or what are his attributes)? What does it mean that God is "sovereign"? It's important to start with these categories because the rest of the study of theology flows from them.

1. What questions have you asked about the Bible? Have you ever been tempted to doubt the trustworthiness of the Bible? Why or why not?

2. Why might it be good to begin our study of theology with the doctrine of Scripture? How is this a foundational doctrine for all the rest of our study?

3. Does it intimidate you to study God specifically? Why is it important for us to understand that there will always be limits to our understanding of God?

DOCTRINE OF MAN AND DOCTRINE OF SIN

Review pages 9–10 in *Knowing God's Truth*

The doctrine of *man* (also called biblical anthropology) deals with questions about humanity, and particularly what it means that men and women were created by God in his image. This doctrine naturally leads to the next category: the doctrine of *sin* (also called hamartiology). When we dive into this category of theology, we're asking questions about the fall of humanity—and in what sense we can rightly describe men and women as "fallen." We'll discuss the meaning of "total depravity" and how humanity's sinful nature affects life on earth (and creates the need for God's work of salvation through Jesus Christ).

1. Why is it so important to have a biblical perspective on men and women, and particularly on *why* and *how* God created them?

2. Would you say that people today see human beings as basically good or basically evil? Explain your answer.

3. What evidence do you see in the world around you of the fall of mankind into sin? Why is humanity's sinful nature somewhat easy to prove and demonstrate?

DOCTRINE OF CHRIST AND DOCTRINE OF SALVATION

Review pages 11–12 in *Knowing God's Truth*

The doctrine of *Christ* (also called Christology) focuses specifically on Jesus—the second person of the Trinity. Key discussions about this doctrine include Jesus's full divinity (he is completely God and always has been) and his full humanity (he truly became human in order to offer himself in the place of sinful human beings to bring them salvation). This doctrine leads naturally to the doctrine of *salvation* (also called soteriology), which includes discussions of Jesus's work on the cross and his resurrection for the sake of saving God's people. These doctrines are incredibly important, rich, and complex; they are also beautiful, for in them we consider the work of Jesus Christ to redeem lost sinners and make them children of God forever.

1. What are some misunderstandings that people today have about Jesus? Why is it important to be clear on who he is—both in his divinity and in his humanity?

2. How might the doctrine of salvation (understanding how a sinner can be saved eternally) impact our lives practically?

3. What questions have you wrestled with about salvation? How are you tempted to doubt that God can save you or to trust things other than Jesus for your salvation?

DOCTRINE OF HEAVEN AND HELL

Review pages 13–14 in *Knowing God's Truth*

In our study of theology, we need to wrestle with what the Bible teaches about *heaven and hell*—the final judgment and future that lies ahead of every human being who has ever lived. We'll consider questions about resurrection life and the new heaven and new earth, as well as the reality of hell as a place of God's perfectly just wrath against sin.

1. What are some commonly held cultural beliefs about heaven? Why might many people today question the existence of a literal hell?

2. Why might the idea of eternal existence in heaven be a difficult concept for some to embrace?

3. What might the existence of hell as a place of eternal punishment teach us about sin and the character of God?

DOCTRINE OF THE CHURCH

Review pages 15–16 in *Knowing God's Truth*

After making our way through the doctrines of God, sin, and salvation (and a few others), we will come to the doctrine of the *church* (also called ecclesiology). We'll again ground our discussion in Scripture as we see the biblical foundations for the church, what purpose it serves, and how it is meant to be governed and led. Within the context of the church, we'll then turn to the *sacraments*, which, in the Protestant tradition, include only the Lord's Supper and baptism. We'll consider what these sacraments symbolize—and how they are meant to glorify Jesus and strengthen his people (and we'll also explain some different perspectives within the Protestant tradition).

1. Why might some people today think that they can have a personal relationship with Jesus without being involved in a church? What could be problematic about that mindset?

2. What questions do you have about the role of the church in the life of a Christian? What different church traditions have you been a part of?

3. How do different church traditions practice baptism? Why might these differences exist? What is your understanding of the reason why we practice the Lord's Supper (or "Communion")?

DOCTRINE OF ANGELS AND DEMONS

Review pages 16–17 in *Knowing God's Truth*

The Bible is clear about the reality of the spiritual realm—that both angels and demons (and a personal devil—Satan) exist as spiritual beings that were created by God for his glorious and eternal purposes. Part of the discipline of theology is coming to understand what the Bible teaches about these spiritual beings and their God-ordained purposes. We also can learn much about the character of our God by considering these beings. Christians need to make sure they are not embracing cultural myths or false ideas about angels and demons, but rather rooting their understanding of these creatures in the clear teachings of Scripture.

1. In what contexts today do people talk about angels—if at all?

2. Why is it important to understand the spiritual realm (angels, demons, Satan) within the context of God as the Creator and all-powerful one?

3. How are people's perceptions and ideas about angels and demons often shaped more by culture (books, movies, stories) than by God's word?

DOCTRINE OF LAST THINGS

Review pages 17–19 in *Knowing God's Truth*

As we approach the end of our study of systematic theology, we'll turn to the doctrine of *last things* (often called eschatology). The "apocalyptic" passages in Scripture (passages in which mysteries are *revealed*, particularly about future things) will be our main focus as we discuss this topic. We'll consider what we can know for sure—according to Scripture—about Jesus's return, the final judgment, and the end of the world. But we'll also acknowledge some different perspectives that faithful Christians have about these things. There are firm convictions and beliefs that every Bible-believing Christian should have about the last days, even though there is some room for disagreement.

1. What do people in your circles generally say and believe about the end of the world (if they talk about it at all)?

2. Why is it important to form at least some belief and understanding about the return of Jesus Christ and the eternal future ahead of us?

3. How can Christians focus on the return of Jesus and the final judgment while also staying focused on obeying God and living a faithful life right now?

DOCTRINE OF THE HOLY SPIRIT

Review pages 19–20 in *Knowing God's Truth*

For many Christians, the most mysterious and least understood of the three persons of the Trinity is the third person—God the Holy Spirit. We tend to have a better understanding of the Father and the Son than we do of the Spirit (who is fully God and a distinct person from the Father and the Son). We need to search the Scriptures to understand the Holy Spirit well—his identity, purpose, and distinct function among the actions and roles of the persons of the Trinity.

1. What questions do you have about the identity and role of the Holy Spirit? Why might this person of the Trinity be the most mysterious to many Christians?

2. Why is it so important to understand the Trinity (God in three persons), as much as we are able, through the study of God's word? How can understanding more about God help us love and worship him more?

3. What ideas about the Holy Spirit have you heard (or been taught) that you have questioned? How might the Holy Spirit be misunderstood in some circles today?

▼ SO WHAT?

As you get ready to dive into your study of basic theology, jot down some answers to the following application questions:

1. How have you grown already in your understanding of the *relevance* of studying theology for the way you think, speak, and live? Why does what you believe and understand about God make a practical difference in your life?

2. What category or topic of theology is of most interest to you? Why?

3. What are some ways you can be asking God to teach you through this study and help you grow in your love for Jesus?

THE DOCTRINE OF SCRIPTURE

The doctrine of Scripture is absolutely fundamental to the discipline of systematic theology. This is because the Bible is the foundation for everything we know about God; it's his revelation to us as human beings. Without the Bible, the whole discipline of doing theology ("God talk") would be pointless and futile. We wouldn't know where to begin—and our ideas about God could come only from our own minds! But we have the great privilege of worshiping a God who *speaks* to us through his written and inspired word: the Bible. Therefore, we have a firm foundation for doing theology. So we start in Scripture—and that means it's good to start by getting clear on what Scripture *is*.

As you get started in this chapter, write down answers to at least some of these initial questions:

1. If you have friends who are not Christians, how might they view the Bible? What comments have you heard unbelievers make about Scripture—if they talk about it at all?

2. Why is it such a gift to us that our Creator God has *spoken* to us through his word? How do you sometimes take that gift for granted?

3. What questions do you have about the Bible—its formation, trustworthiness, or unity?

BEGINNING WITH GOD'S WORD

Review pages 25–27 in *Knowing God's Truth*

Certain passages in Scripture (such as Rom. 1:18–20 and Ps. 19) teach us that we can grasp some *basic* knowledge about God (his existence, his power, etc.) through the beauty and majesty of creation. We can look around our world and say, "Wow! This is amazing. There must be a huge, glorious Creator who made all this!" Because creation teaches us about God in this way, it is sometimes called "general revelation." But the Bible is also clear that we need God's "special revelation"—his word—in order to know him personally, find forgiveness for our sins, and be saved through the work of his Son. This is why we start our study of theology with the Bible—God's special revelation to us.

1. Write about a time when you were in awe of some aspect of God's creation (an ocean, a mountain, etc.). How did that sense of awe create in you an awareness of God as Creator?

2. What truths about God (or about human beings) are *not* immediately obvious just by looking at the wonder of creation? Why do we need God's special revelation?

3. How are you doing—right now—in your personal reading and study of the Bible? How could you grow in this area?

WHAT SCRIPTURE TELLS US ABOUT GOD

Review pages 27–29 in *Knowing God's Truth*

What does the very fact that the Bible exists tell us about God? It tells us that he is a *speaking* God. He wants to communicate with us—and he wants us to listen to him! God is not a distant or removed deity who set things in motion and then stepped away from his creation. No—God speaks to the people he has created. He wants to be known. He wants us to relate to him. The existence of God's *word* tells us a lot about the God who made us.

1. "Deism" is a belief that there is a God, but he is merely the Creator—not one who is intimately involved with his creation. How does the existence of the Bible (God's word) steer us away from a deistic view of God?

2. Why should we see God's communication with human beings as an act of his grace and mercy toward us?

3. What does the existence of the Bible imply about God's hope for a relationship with human beings? Why is this good news?

ASPECTS OF THE DOCTRINE OF SCRIPTURE
The Inspiration of Scripture

Review pages 29–31 in *Knowing God's Truth*

The apostle Paul writes, "All Scripture is breathed out by God and profitable for teaching, for reproof, for correction, and for training in righteousness, that the man of God may be complete, equipped for every good work" (2 Tim. 3:16–17). The doctrine of the *inspiration* of the Bible refers to Scripture being "breathed out" by God through the power of the Holy Spirit. God the Holy Spirit *inspired* the human authors of the Bible to write exactly what God wanted them to write. So the Bible is a human book (written by human authors) *and* a divine book (fully inspired by God).

1. In what sense is the Bible is a human book? What role did the human authors have in writing down the words of Scripture?

_____

_____

_____

2. Why is it so important for us to understand the Bible as a divine book—completely inspired by God himself? What difference should that make in the way we read it and study it?

_____

_____

_____

3. How should the doctrine of inspiration increase our trust in the Bible—and our respect for it?

_____

_____

_____

The Authority of Scripture

Review pages 31–33 in _Knowing God's Truth_

One continuous theme throughout the Bible is that God rules his people _by his word_. This reminds us of something important about Scripture: as God's word, it has _authority_ in the lives of God's people. The Bible doesn't only teach us truths about our world, ourselves, and God; it is meant to rule over us and guide our lives with authority and power. Where the Bible speaks, God speaks—and this means that Scripture is our final authority.

1. How does the authority of the Bible make it different from any other book in the world?

2. How does understanding the Bible's authority change the way we read it and study it? Why should we always be asking application questions when we read the Bible, in addition to questions about interpretation?

3. What does God's rule over his people by his word teach you about God? How does he want you to view and approach his word?

THE DOCTRINE OF SCRIPTURE

The Clarity of Scripture

Review pages 34–35 in *Knowing God's Truth*

The doctrine of the *clarity* of Scripture is also sometimes called the "perspicuity" of Scripture. This doctrine doesn't mean that everything in the Bible is easy to understand; there are certainly difficult and confusing parts, as you probably have noticed! But the basic truths about God, human beings, sin, and salvation are *sufficiently clear* in Scripture that someone who reads it will be able to understand what he or she needs to know about how to follow God by faith. Isn't this good news? The Bible is *clear*. While we won't understand everything in it right away, we can know what we need to know in order to believe and be saved.

1. What does the clarity of Scripture *not* mean—in terms of parts that may confuse or puzzle us?

2. What are some of the basic, fundamental truths in the Bible that are extremely *clear*—even though we may still wrestle with other parts of it?

3. Why is it good news that the Bible is clear when it comes to our understanding of God—and our hope for salvation?

The Infallibility of Scripture

Review pages 36–37 in *Knowing God's Truth*

In answer to the question "Can we trust the Bible?" we turn to the doctrine of the Bible's *infallibility*. To say that the Bible is infallible is to say that it is without fault; it will not deceive us or lead us astray because it speaks accurately, faithfully, and truthfully about everything it addresses. This obviously does *not* mean that the Bible speaks to every subject in the world; the Bible doesn't teach algebra or U.S. history, for example! But when it speaks, it speaks infallibly.

1. Why is it so important for Christians to know that they can trust the Bible?

2. What are some examples of truths, facts, or types of information that the Bible does not address?

3. Have you heard people attack the infallibility of Scripture? What kinds of claims do such people make? How might you begin to respond to them?

The Power of Scripture

Review pages 38–39 in _Knowing God's Truth_

Our words as human beings have a kind of power—power to wound, encourage, correct, or inform. God's word, though, has a different kind of power: intrinsic power to create, change, and transform. It's important to understand that God's written and inspired word—the Bible—is powerful in this way! God works powerfully through his word to confront, convict, and rebuke—and through the hearing of his inspired word, God regularly brings repentance and faith in Jesus his Son. God's word has power unlike the words of any human being.

1. Read 2 Timothy 3:16–17 again. If God's word truly is powerful, what effects should we expect it to have on people's lives when they study it and hear it preached and taught?

2. How have you experienced the power of God's word in your own life—convicting, shaping, and changing you?

3. Why should the truth about the power of God's word strengthen your confidence in the Bible—and your witness to unbelievers through the use of the Bible?

RESPONDING TO THE DOCTRINE OF SCRIPTURE

Review pages 40–41 in _Knowing God's Truth_

If all of these things are true about Scripture, how should we respond? We should commit to studying God's word carefully, living under its authority (being guided by the Bible in everything), and knowing it as well as we possibly can. If the Bible really is the word of our God, we need to commit to building our lives upon it!

1. Have you been convicted about being too "laid back" in your approach to God's word? Why might we tend to take the Bible for granted?

2. Read Isaiah 66:1–2. What are some ways that you could more humbly and diligently study, know, and learn God's word?

3. How might you tell if the Bible is really the shaping and guiding influence in your life?

THE BIBLE AND SYSTEMATIC THEOLOGY

Review pages 42–43 in *Knowing God's Truth*

Now that we've discussed all of these wonderful truths and doctrines about Scripture, we come back to our study of theology. Here's the point: the study of systematic theology always must be grounded in God's word. We need to be careful that our thoughts about God, sin, human beings, and salvation never become disconnected from God's clear revelation in his written and inspired word. All along the way in our study of theology, we are going to be grounding every part of the conversation in God's revelation of himself in Scripture.

1. Read Isaiah 66:1–2 one more time (and memorize it if you can). How can you respond to God's word with more humility, respect, and even "trembling"?

2. What are the dangers of doing theology (thinking thoughts about God) in a way that is disconnected from God's word?

3. Why has it been helpful to start our study of theology with the doctrine of Scripture?

_____

_____

_____

▼ SO WHAT?

As you conclude this chapter, jot down answers to the following application questions:

1. What was new to you in this chapter in terms of truths about the Bible?

_____

_____

_____

2. What was most convicting to you regarding your general attitude and approach toward God's word?

_____

_____

_____

3. How should your confidence in God's word be strengthened after studying this topic of systematic theology? How can you expect the Bible to work in your life and the lives of others?

_____

_____

_____

THE DOCTRINE OF GOD

A. W. Tozer once said, "What comes into our minds when we think about God is the most important thing about us" (*The Knowledge of the Holy*). If this is true, then what we are about to study in this chapter should not be taken lightly. We are, on the basis and foundation of Scripture, going to begin forming right thoughts about the only true God of the universe. This is the God who created us. He is the God who has made himself known in Scripture. What we think and believe about this eternal being is the most important thing about us!

Write down brief answers to the following questions as you prepare to dive into this chapter:

1. What was your first thought when you read the above quotation from Tozer? Do you regard your "theology" as the "most important thing" about you?

_____

_____

_____

_____

2. Why is the way we think about God so incredibly important?

_____

_____

_____

_____

3. What comes into your mind when you think about God? Describe the vision and characteristics of God that you have formed in your mind.

_____

_____

_____

_____

4. Do you think that your thoughts about God need some work and improvement? Why or why not?

_____

_____

_____

_____

WHAT IS GOD?

Review pages 49–51 in *Knowing God's Truth*

God is *spirit*—so he is omnipresent and invisible to human eyes. God is absolutely and perfectly glorious, holy, and "other," so that an encounter with him would be absolutely overwhelming for sinful human beings. Remember, though, that while God the Father and God the Holy Spirit do not have physical bodies, God the Son (Jesus Christ) *does* have one, which he took on when he came to earth and will have forever.

1. Why is it important to remember that God is spirit? What attributes of God are connected to his existence as a spirit?

2. How do human beings sometimes forget the holiness of God? Why is this such an important and foundational truth about God?

3. Read Revelation 4:8, 11. What do these verses teach you about God's being and what he is like?

THE TRINITY—GOD AS THREE IN ONE

Review pages 52–54 in *Knowing God's Truth*

The one true God has existed eternally as one God in three persons—the Father, the Son, and the Holy Spirit. The persons of the Trinity exist in perfect unity and without any confusion. This doctrine of the Trinity is clearly taught in the Bible, although the term *Trinity* is not actually used. We can summarize the Bible's teaching about the Trinity with these six simple statements: the Father is God; the Son is God; the Spirit is God;

the Father is not the Son or the Spirit; the Son is not the Father or the Spirit; and the Spirit is not the Father or the Son.

1. What is mysterious about the doctrine of the Trinity? Why do human analogies and metaphors tend to fail to capture the essence of the Trinity?

2. From what you know already about the Bible, what are some specific roles that seem to be accomplished by God the Father? God the Son? God the Holy Spirit?

3. Read 1 Peter 1:1–2. How does Peter reference the three persons of the Trinity in his greeting? What do we learn about his understanding of God in three persons?

THE ETERNALITY AND ASEITY OF GOD

Review pages 55–56 in *Knowing God's Truth*

God is eternal; he had no beginning and will have no end. Remember that since God has existed eternally, he must be perfectly satisfied in himself. This doctrine is known as God's "aseity"; it refers to the fact that God has no need of anyone or anything, but is completely satisfied in himself—and has been from eternity past. Therefore, he must have created the world and saved his people out of the gracious overflow of his joy, love, and grace—not to satisfy anything lacking in his identity or his satisfaction.

1. Why does thinking about the concept of eternity seem to hurt our brains? How can it be good for us, spiritually, to think about the mysterious ways, being, and eternality of God? How does such thinking help us see ourselves rightly?

2. Why is it such good news that God did not create us or save us because he *needs* us, but rather out of the overflow of his joy, love, and grace?

3. Read Acts 17:24–25. What does Paul say about what God needs from people? What can we conclude about God's gracious heart toward sinners who cannot give him anything?

THE JUSTICE OF GOD

Review pages 57–58 in *Knowing God's Truth*

God is perfectly and completely just, righteous, and true. His perfect justice demands that he punish sin perfectly and completely, because if he did not, he would cease to be God. But here is the good news of the gospel: God's justice was *perfectly satisfied* at the cross, where Jesus took the full penalty of sin in the place of God's people. The way in which our salvation was accomplished shows us the perfect justice (punishing sin) and grace (saving sinners) of our God.

1. The fact that God is perfectly just can be frightening—especially as we realize we are sinners who deserve punishment. Have you experienced this fear? Why or why not?

2. Why is it so important to remember that sinners are saved through an act of God's *justice* at the cross, as well as through God's grace?

3. Read Romans 3:21–26. What are some of the words Paul uses to describe what happened for us—through Jesus—at the cross? How does he explain God's justice in his salvation through his Son?

THE GRACE OF GOD

Review pages 59–60 in *Knowing God's Truth*

God revealed himself to Moses in Exodus 34:6 as "merciful and gracious, slow to anger, and abounding in steadfast love and faithfulness." God is perfectly gracious, even offering salvation to sinners through the death of his Son on the cross. God, even now, is gracious and patient, delaying the return of Christ so that more people have time to repent and be saved. This truth about God is good news for any sinner who will repent and turn to Jesus in faith!

1. If God were perfectly just, but not perfectly gracious, where would that leave us? What would all sinners rightly deserve and receive from God?

2. Why should God's grace be so amazing to us when we understand rightly who we are—and who he is?

3. Read Ephesians 2:1–10. Who were we before God's grace took hold of us and saved us (vv. 1–3)? How are we saved—and why is this such good news (vv. 4–10)?

THE SOVEREIGNTY OF GOD

Review pages 61–63 in *Knowing God's Truth*

The Bible clearly teaches that God is completely sovereign—powerfully and personally controlling and ruling over the universe he created. God is constantly working out his sovereign plan in his intended way, even when we don't see it or understand it. God's sovereignty extends to our salvation, although the Bible clearly presents human beings as responsible creatures who make real choices.

1. What does God's sovereignty tell you about his power? How does God become "bigger" in our minds and hearts?

2. Why is it so difficult to fit together God's sovereignty with human responsibility? Can you think of some examples where the Bible holds these truths in tension?

3. Read Ephesians 1:3–6, where Paul describes the salvation of the Christians to whom he writes. When does he say God's plan of salvation for them began?

_____

_____

THE GLORY OF GOD

Review pages 63–65 in _Knowing God's Truth_

The glorious Creator and Redeemer God ultimately is pursuing his own glory. God's glory refers to his worthiness, honor, praise, and fame in all the universe. Remember, though, that God's glory beautifully and perfectly matches up with our greatest good as his people. This is good news, because God is glorified in saving sinners and giving them an inheritance (see Eph. 1:11–14). When God chases his glory, he also chases our greatest eternal good!

1. Why is God's pursuit of his own glory not a selfish or prideful pursuit—as it would be for a human being?

_____

_____

_____

_____

2. How does God's glory line up with what is best for us as his people?

_____

_____

_____

_____

3. Read Ephesians 1:11–14. What does Paul say about the glory of God?

_____

_____

▼ SO WHAT?

As you conclude this chapter, jot down answers to the following application questions:

1. What have you learned in this chapter about the character of God that you hadn't understood or seriously considered before? How will this new understanding change the way you think about God, worship him, and talk to him through prayer?

2. What is still mysterious to you about God's character, being, and ways? Why is it OK to not understand God exhaustively and completely?

3. How are you encouraged by who God is? Why are his just and gracious character and ways good news for sinners?

Chapter 4

THE DOCTRINE OF MAN

The doctrine of man is also commonly referred to as "biblical anthropology." In this chapter, we try to bring together the core teachings of the Bible about human beings—who they are, where they come from, what they are like, and what their purpose is. Our study of this category of systematic theology begins in the earliest chapters of Scripture, with the creation of Adam and Eve (the first man and woman) in "the image of God." Human beings are set apart—distinct—from the rest of God's physical creation in this way—they reflect God and were created by God to know, love, worship, and live in relationship with their Creator. We discuss what it means to be made in the image of God, with all of its beautiful implications for understanding human beings, as well as the God who created us!

As you get started with this chapter, jot down answers to the following questions:

1. What are some obvious ways in which human beings are distinct from the rest of the animal kingdom? What deeper mental, emotional, and spiritual capabilities do we possess?

2. Without looking ahead in the chapter, how would you explain what it means for human beings to be made in the image of God?

3. What are some of the immediate implications of the fact that we have a Creator? If God made us, what does that mean for our value, our purpose, and our responsibility?

THE *ORIGINS* OF MAN

Review pages 73–75 in *Knowing God's Truth*

The foundation of our discussion of the doctrine of man is God's role as our Creator. But even more specifically, we want to note the uniqueness of human beings in all of God's created order; there is nothing else like a human being! Adam and Eve—apart from all the rest of the animal kingdom—were given dominion by God to rule over his creation. They were also invited into a special relationship of love and friendship with their God— something that is beautifully unique and gloriously eternal for those who put their faith in God's Son. Human beings are not just another species of mammal—they are uniquely created by God, in his image, and have been given dominion and an eternal purpose.

1. Read Psalm 8. What does this psalm reveal about the wonder of God's creation—and particularly his creation of human beings?

2. Why might some unbelievers insist that human beings are just animals that are not unique from the rest of God's created order?

3. How does the idea of the uniqueness of human beings give special value and responsibility to us as men and women?

THE *ESSENCE* OF MAN
The Image of God (the *Imago Dei*)

Review pages 76–77 in *Knowing God's Truth*

Central to our understanding of human beings is the truth that we are made in the image of God, which is also referred to as the *imago Dei*. While the Bible affirms our creation in this way, it does not define clearly and succinctly what it means—probably because the concept is so beautifully rich and complex. As human beings, we *reflect* our Creator in a multitude of ways. We can have deep relationships with other human beings—and with God. We have an aptitude for worship, belief, faith, hope, and joy. We communicate with one another; we can even communicate with our God through prayer. We have an innate sense of morality—and we naturally desire eternal meaning, joy, and purpose. These are just some of the ways that God's image is reflected in us.

1. Read Genesis 1:26–27. What does the author of Genesis emphasize in these verses about God's creation of human beings?

2. What are some other ways (in addition to the ones mentioned above) that human beings reflect God in a way that animals (or other parts of God's creation) do not?

3. If we are made in God's image, what does that say about the dignity, value, and worth of human beings?

Implications of the *Imago Dei*

Review pages 78–79 in *Knowing God's Truth*

The reality of God's creation of human beings in his image means that every man, woman, and child has eternal worth and value. This truth has implications for the way we treat the people around us, whether they are believers in Jesus Christ or not. Even men and women who reject Jesus, and therefore are not our brothers and sisters in Christ, are our neighbors—and are worthy of respect, dignity, and love by virtue of their creation in God's image. This truth should govern and shape the way we treat people—with humility, grace, love, and honor.

1. How can the reality of human beings' creation in God's image explain our natural desire for meaning and purpose—and our sense that there is "something more" than just this world?

2. Read James 3:1–12 (noting v. 9 especially). What does James command about our attitudes and actions toward human beings, all of whom have been created in the image of God?

3. Why is it so important for us to remind ourselves that the people we pass every day on the street were created in the image of God? What behaviors and attitudes might we avoid if we do this?

The Human Being

Review pages 80–81 in *Knowing God's Truth*

As human beings, we certainly belong to God's physical creation; we walk, run, eat, sleep, stub our toes, and experience pain. But it's clear that we are more than mindless physical beings; we experience joy, sadness, and anger—and we can sing, pray, mourn, and worship! The Bible is clear about the existence of the human *soul*—the inner reality and person-hood that we all have. Sometimes the Bible talks about the *heart* of human beings as well, which, biblically speaking, refers to the inner core of who we are (not the physical beating hearts in our chests!). Human beings, then, have been created by God as both physical and spiritual creatures—and this has implications for how we think about sin and salvation.

1. Read Psalm 16. What aspects of David's personhood are revealed in the way he talks about himself? In other words, how does David reveal that he thinks about himself as more complex than merely a physical body made of matter?

2. What are some of your earliest memories of spiritual awareness—perhaps through guilt, worship, confession, or prayer?

3. How are the physical and spiritual/emotional aspects of our identities wrapped up together and therefore quite interdependent?

The Physical Nature of the Body

Review pages 82–84 in *Knowing God's Truth*

Throughout history, some groups associated with Christianity have tended to emphasize the *spirituality* of human beings to the exclusion of their *physical* bodies. We need to remember that the Bible has a very strong doctrine of physical creation—and tells us of a glorious physical future for both our world and our bodies! The fact that Jesus Christ, God's Son, took on a physical human body—and was physically resurrected after his death on the cross—tells us that our eternal salvation will be physical as well as spiritual. God means to save his people into physical resurrection life. This means that, even now, we must value God's physical creation, including human bodies, for his glory.

1. Read Job 19:25–27. What hope does Job have for the future of his physical body as well as his soul? Why is this encouraging?

2. What dangers might come if we overemphasize our spiritual identities (and spiritual future) while neglecting the importance of our physical identities (and physical future)?

3. How can understanding God's value and love for his physical creation encourage you to care well for your physical body and the physical needs of others?

God's Communicable and Incommunicable Attributes

Review pages 84–86 in *Knowing God's Truth*

As we continue to think about the nature and essence of human beings, it is good to distinguish the ways in which we can and should be like our God, as well as the ways we can never be like him. Theologians call this distinction the *communicable* and *incommunicable* attributes of God. In other words, some attributes of God are "communicated" to us in a way that we can embody, but others are not. There are certainly qualities of God's character that we can imitate: his love, graciousness, patience, kindness, and truthfulness, for example. But, of course, we will never be omniscient (all-knowing), omnipresent (present everywhere), and omnipotent (all-powerful).

1. Read Galatians 5:22–26. What attributes ("fruit") of God are clearly meant to be present and evident in the lives of redeemed human beings?

2. How does the concept of the *imago Dei* ("the image of God") point us to the fact that human beings *should* be like God in some ways?

THE DOCTRINE OF MAN

3. Why must we remember that there will always be a distinction between human beings and the God who created them?

Sin and the Salvation of Man

Review pages 86–88 in *Knowing God's Truth*

While human beings have the glorious privilege of being created in the image of God, they also are born into sin. Ever since sin entered the world through the disobedience of Adam and Eve in the garden of Eden, human beings have been born with both the dignity of the *imago Dei* and the stain of sin, guilt, and a sinful nature—all of which make us eternally guilty before our holy God. God's saving work through Jesus, though, offers grace to fallen human beings who look to Christ by faith. The Bible, then, contains very *bad* news about the human condition (we are all fallen, sinful, and guilty of rebellion against God) as well as very *good* news about God's saving plan for humans (he sent his Son, Jesus, through whom sinners can be saved by faith).

1. Read Ephesians 2:1–10 again (you read this also in the last chapter). What do the first three verses tell us about human beings' spiritual state apart from God's grace? What is the good news about God's salvation of sinful human beings (vv. 4–10)?

2. Why is it unpopular today to talk about sin, judgment, guilt, and death? How does the Bible clearly tell us about our eternal condition apart from Jesus, and why is it important for us to understand this?

3. What does God's saving plan, through Jesus, tell us about his love and value for the human beings he created, despite their sin?

THE *PURPOSE* AND *END* OF MAN

Review pages 89–90 in *Knowing God's Truth*

Given what we've already discussed about human beings—their creation in the image of God, their spiritual and physical natures, and so on—one conclusion we must draw is that human beings were created by God for *eternity*. In God's perfect wisdom, he made men and women in his image—for his glory—and designed them to live forever. This is a staggering thing to think about! The gracious invitation from God to sinful human beings is to repent, place their faith in Jesus Christ, and be welcomed into the enjoyment of God for all eternity to come. This is the great gospel destiny for all who will believe in Jesus.

1. Read Psalm 16 one more time. How does David point forward to the ultimate, eternal destiny of human beings who place their faith in God?

2. How is it obvious that many people today think only about this earthly life—and not about eternity ahead? Why is that kind of thinking dangerous?

3. What is your reaction to the idea of "enjoying" God? Does that make sense to you? Why or why not?

SO WHAT?

As you conclude this chapter, jot down answers to the following application questions:

1. What was new to you in this chapter with regard to God's creation of and intention for human beings?

2. How might some of the truths of this chapter lead you toward more respect, esteem, and value for your fellow human beings?

3. Why is it important to consider God's eternal intention and destiny for the people he has made? How can doing so encourage us to embrace the gospel and believe in Jesus?

THE DOCTRINE OF SIN

While it is tempting to rush toward a discussion of the doctrine of salvation, it's important for us to first spend time rightly understanding a very important theological category: *sin*. To put it very simply, we need to understand the *bad* news about ourselves before we can really and fully understand the *good* news about what God has done for us through the person and work of Jesus Christ. The doctrine of sin is so important because it helps us rightly understand ourselves (as well as the world around us) so that we can better understand our God—and his grace and love toward us.

Jot down some answers to these questions as you get started with this chapter:

1. How would you define *sin*?

2. As you look around the world, what effects of sin do you see today? How does sin damage individuals and their relationships with one another?

3. Why do some people in the world today not like to label sin as sin? What are some other ways that people like to talk about sin?

WHAT IS SIN?

Review pages 95–96 in *Knowing God's Truth*

Sin is, essentially, *any lack of conformity to the perfect will and character of God.* This is a very broad definition—probably much broader than the way you often think about sin. When we hear the word *sin*, we often think of seriously wrong actions, such as violence, theft, or extreme lies. But sin is more basic and widespread than these actions. Sin is *any deviation from God's perfect will and character.* It is anything that is out of step with who God is. This means that sin in our world is opposed to the character of God; it can happen in lots of ways—and it's everywhere!

1. How do many people today react to the idea of sin? Do you think that most people think of themselves as sinners? Why or why not?

2. Why is it so important to connect our definition and understanding of sin to the character of God? How does it help us to see bad things (sin) in relation to the ultimate good thing (God)?

3. What evidence in the world today (or in your life) can you point to in order to prove the reality of sin?

THE *ORIGIN* OF SIN

Review pages 97–100 in *Knowing God's Truth*

Originally, when God created the world and placed Adam and Eve in the garden of Eden to tend and keep it, there was no sin. Adam and Eve—the first man and woman—walked obediently with God in perfect fellowship, love, and joy. This didn't last forever, though. Satan (also part of God's creation) rebelled against God's word—then sneaked into the garden disguised as a serpent with the devious intention of turning Adam and Eve toward sinful rebellion as well. Satan questioned God's good commands and then blatantly denied God's word. Eve and Adam listened to the lies of the serpent and disobeyed God. With that, sin entered the world, and God's good creation became fallen—infected by sin in every part.

1. Read Genesis 3:1–7. What do you notice about the conversation that led to the first act of disobedience to God's word? How was Eve, and then Adam, tempted toward sin?

2. Why is sin so often accompanied by a false view of God or a twisting of the truth of his word?

3. While God does not sin and does not cause people to sin, he created Satan and sovereignly ordained for the entrance of sin into his good creation. Why are these two truths so difficult for human beings to grasp?

THE *EFFECTS* OF SIN

Review pages 100–102 in *Knowing God's Truth*

After the first sin of Adam and Eve, life became much more difficult for human beings. Sin invaded not just human hearts, but every aspect of God's world. The ground was cursed because of sin, making it difficult for human beings to work and survive. The pain of childbirth came into the world for the first time. And *death* itself became a part of this fallen world, as the just consequence of human rebellion and disobedience to God. Every human being born after Adam and Eve has died or will die. We face not only physical death but also eternal spiritual death (the punishment of hell), unless God grants us saving faith in his Son, Jesus Christ. The effects of sin are far-reaching and extremely deadly.

1. Read Romans 5:12–21. What came into the world—and to human beings—through Adam and his sin? What comes through Jesus to all who believe in him?

2. Why is it just and right that when human beings created by the infinitely holy God sin against him, they deserve to be punished by death?

3. How does an understanding of the seriousness of sin help us make sense of the pain, sickness, disease, and death in our world today? How can God use these things to point us toward himself?

Guilt and Wrath

Review pages 102–4 in *Knowing God's Truth*

Sin not only brought death into our world, but it also made every human being guilty before the holy God and deserving of his wrath (righteous anger against sin). These terms—*guilt* and *wrath*—are not popular in our world today because many people prefer to think of human beings as basically good and of God as a loving being who never gets angry. The biblical truth, though, is that God's perfect holiness and love *demand* his wrath against sin; God would not be just and perfect if he did not hate and punish evil! Every human being born into this world inherits Adam and Eve's guilt—and is under the wrath of God because of sin.

1. Read Romans 1:18–32. How does Paul explain the effects of God's wrath, which he has poured out on the world because of human sin? How does sin lead to even more sin?

2. What seems unfair about the idea of humans being born guilty before God and under his wrath? Does this concept make more sense as we think more deeply about God's perfect holiness, goodness, and righteousness?

3. What aspects of God's character make his wrath against sin necessary?

Sinful Natures

Review pages 104–6 in *Knowing God's Truth*

Because of the sin of Adam and Eve, every human being born into this world after them has had a *sin nature*. In other words, all people are prone to sin; they sin naturally because doing so is in accord with who they actually are. We all know this by experience; as much as we may try to be perfect (or even just good), we mess up. We say cruel things. We deceive. We harbor anger and envy in our hearts. The reality of the sinful nature means that we have no choice *but* to sin!

1. Read Psalm 51:1–5, noting the way David talks about his sin. How do these verses point to the reality of a sinful nature in every human being?

2. How does our sinful nature explain the struggle inside of us when we try to do good, to obey, or to be nice to people we don't like?

3. What are some signs of the reality of a sinful nature from our youngest years?

Total Depravity

Review pages 106–8 in *Knowing God's Truth*

When we talk about "total depravity," we mean that human beings are completely sinful and fallen in every way—in every aspect of their being. The word *depravity* refers to fallenness, sin, and ungodliness. *Total* depravity, then, implies that we are completely fallen—and therefore totally separated from God. It does not mean that we are as bad as we possibly could be, but rather that no part of us (mental, physical, or emotional) is exempt from the effects of sin and the fall. Sin has touched and infected every part of who we are as human beings.

1. Read Genesis 6:5–6. How do these verses describe the depths of sin into which humanity had fallen? How might this description help us understand what it means to be depraved (i.e., completely fallen and lacking any good)?

2. What are some ways in which human bodies have been affected by the fall? How does our sinful nature affect us emotionally?

3. If every aspect of who we are is affected by sin and therefore depraved, what does that imply about our ability to save ourselves?

Propitiation

Review pages 109–11 in *Knowing God's Truth*

We have learned about the holiness of God, our sinfulness as human beings (our guilt, sinful natures, and total depravity), and the just wrath of God that hangs over us because of our sin. This introduces the need for an important aspect of the saving work of God through Jesus Christ: *propitiation*. Propitiation refers to the way in which God's wrath against our sin was poured out on Jesus at the cross so that it was satisfied (propitiated). The cross was a place of grace and mercy toward sinners, but it was also a place where God's full justice was on display. Sin was fully paid for; the wrath of God against his people's sin was propitiated as Jesus bore it on the cross in their place.

1. Read 1 John 4:10. How does John connect God's act of propitiation to his love for sinful human beings?

2. How does the reality of propitiation (and the need for it) teach us about the character of God (both his love and his holiness)?

3. Why can the doctrine of propitiation be incredibly encouraging for you as a sinner who looks to Jesus by faith? How can it help to assure you of your salvation?

Christians and Sin

Review pages 111–13 in *Knowing God's Truth*

Christians have confidence that the *penalty* for their sin really has been paid in full. Followers of Jesus will face no punishment for their sin. This simple fact should be a great motivation for forgiven sinners to live lives of obedience to their gracious Savior. But as Paul points out in Romans 6, the good news for Christians is not just that the penalty for sin has been paid, but also that the *power* of sin in their lives is gone. Apart from Christ, every person in the world is not just a sinner but a "slave" to sin. Unbelievers have no choice but to sin; they are enslaved to it. But the Holy Spirit dwells within Christians and gives them power to say no to sin.

1. Read Romans 6:1–14. How does Paul respond to the implied suggestion that sinners saved by grace should not worry about sin but can keep on sinning because God will always be gracious to them?

2. Why is it important to acknowledge that Christians sometimes still sin? How should Christians respond when they struggle with sin?

3. What kind of attitude should a genuine Christian have toward his or her sin?

THE *ULTIMATE DEFEAT* OF SIN

Review pages 113–15 in *Knowing God's Truth*

Even though, for Christians, the penalty of sin has been paid, the power of sin is broken, and the pleasure of sin has begun to disappear, we still will struggle with sin for the rest of our lives. Christians are to be more and more sanctified (made more holy and more like Jesus) by the power of the Holy Spirit and through their own obedience and discipline. But the process of sanctification will not be perfectly completed in this life. One day, though, the *presence* of sin in our lives—and in our world—will be finally eradicated. Sin will be destroyed, Satan will be defeated, and we will be made perfect—physically and spiritually—to live forever in the new heaven and new earth with Jesus, our Lord and Savior.

1. Read Revelation 21:5–8, 22–27. What do these verses tell us about the experience that is ahead for Christians in eternity to come? What kind of things will disappear forever?

2. How should Christians approach sin in their lives? Why should God's grace to us in Jesus inspire us to attack sin and put it to death—and fight temptation by the power of the Holy Spirit?

3. Why should the eternal future you have ahead of you in Christ encourage you? What do you have to look forward to for thousands and millions of years to come?

SO WHAT?

As you conclude this chapter, jot down answers to the following application questions:

1. What were some new concepts or lessons about sin that you learned in this chapter? How were these discoveries helpful to you?

2. How does the doctrine of sin help you better understand the current state of the world around you—with regard to both human beings and the wider creation?

3. In what ways should a deeper understanding of the doctrine of sin lead you to a greater appreciation of God's grace?

Chapter 6

THE DOCTRINE OF JESUS CHRIST

We are now going to focus on the doctrine of Jesus Christ—sometimes called Christology. Of course, we have talked about Jesus in every chapter of *Knowing God's Truth* so far; he is absolutely essential to every topic and category of study in systematic theology! Still, it is necessary (and practiced by most theologians) to devote an entire theological category to Christology. Precisely because Jesus is so central to everything else we study in systematic theology, we need to be clear on who he is, what he accomplished, and all he means to God's people and God's creation.

As you get started, jot down answers to the following questions:

1. What questions do you bring to the table about Jesus Christ—his person, identity, or work?

2. How do people around you who do not know Jesus personally tend to think about him? Why might they respect him? What aspects of his identity—or which of his claims—might they reject?

JESUS AND HIS IMPACT

Review pages 119–20 in *Knowing God's Truth*

It's hard to exaggerate the impact that Jesus—the man—has had on world history for the past two thousand years. Entire cultures have been shaped through the influence of Jesus and his teachings. And here's something very important to remember: Christianity, unlike any other world religion, will rise and fall on the existence, death, and resurrection of its founder. In other words, Christianity is all about a *person*—Jesus Christ. Islam could exist without the prophet Muhammad; Hinduism could exist without its founder; Buddhism, as a system, could technically exist without the Buddha. Christianity, though, could not exist without Jesus; he is the very center and substance of Christian belief—God in human flesh, the crucified Savior, and the risen Lord.

1. How might some people try to separate Christian morality or teaching from the person and work of Jesus Christ? Why is that not ultimately possible?

2. What are some ways in which Jesus and his teachings have shaped or affected the culture you live in today?

3. If Jesus were not alive today, how would that affect your perspective on Christianity, especially in relationship to other world religions?

JESUS'S *IDENTITY*
Eternal Existence

Review pages 121–23 in *Knowing God's Truth*

Before time began, throughout eternity past (a concept that we cannot fully grasp with our human minds), Jesus has existed as the second person of the Trinity, which we learned about in previous chapters. This is the word that we use to describe the God of the Bible, who presents himself to us as one God in three persons: the Father, the Son, and the Holy Spirit. Along with the Father and the Spirit, Jesus (God the Son) was active in the creation of all things. But Jesus was not always *human.* There was a certain point in time—about two thousand years ago—when the eternally existent second person of the Trinity took on flesh and became a man.

1. Read John 1:1–18. What do these verses tell us about the role of Jesus in creation? What do they tell us about his eternal existence, as well as his identity as God?

2. Why is it so important to remember that Jesus has existed eternally—that he is uncreated?

3. How should remembering Jesus's role in creation expand your view of him? Why is it so amazing that the eternally existent Son of God also became a human man?

True Humanity

Review pages 123–26 in *Knowing God's Truth*

Through the miraculous work of the Holy Spirit, God made Mary pregnant with a baby—and Jesus, the eternally existent Son of God, became human. This doctrine is often called the "incarnation"—the moment when Jesus took on human flesh. We need to remember that Jesus did not just *appear* to be human; he really *became* human—like us in every way, except that he did not have a sinful nature and never sinned. The incarnation reminds us that Jesus can sympathize with us, for he lived a human life and walked on earth as a real man. Also, the fact that Jesus truly became human means that he could truly be a substitute for human beings on the cross. He became like us so that he could save us!

1. Read Hebrews 2:14–18. What aspects of Jesus's humanity are emphasized in these verses? How can the reality of Jesus's humanity encourage and help us as his people today?

2. What is mysterious about the incarnation of Jesus Christ? What aspects of it are still difficult for you to understand?

3. Why is it so important for our salvation that Jesus truly became human? Why is it good news that Jesus will *remain* fully human (and fully God) for all eternity to come?

Heresies about Jesus

Review pages 126–28 in *Knowing God's Truth*

Historically, many heresies (dangerous false teachings) have been built on assumptions that Jesus was either not quite fully human or not quite fully God. As you can tell from our discussion of Christology so far, we are intent on affirming that the Bible teaches two truths about Jesus extremely clearly: Jesus was, and is, fully *human*, and he was, and is, fully *God*. One ancient heresy, Docetism, taught that Jesus only *seemed* to be human, but was really not. Another heresy, Arianism, taught that Jesus was not fully God, but was a powerful being *created* by the Father. Faithful Christianity has always affirmed that Jesus Christ is fully God and fully human in one person.

1. Read Philippians 2:5–11. What do these verses tell us about Jesus's humble descent, in which he took on humanity? What do they tell us about Jesus's ultimate exaltation?

2. Why might some people veer toward false teachings that present Jesus as not fully human?

3. Why might some people veer toward false teachings that present Jesus as not fully God?

JESUS'S *SAVING WORK*
Suffering and Death

Review pages 128–30 in *Knowing God's Truth*

Jesus Christ really, physically died. While it's not right to say that God himself died (or else he would have ceased to be God!)—Jesus, in his humanity, truly experienced real death. Jesus also experienced immense physical suffering, being whipped, beaten, and nailed to a cross by his hands and feet. Even so, the greatest suffering that Jesus experienced was the agony of being under the wrath of God the Father. He was treated like a sinner by God himself, and he bore the terrible pain of separation from God, which is hell itself. Jesus went through all that in order to save God's people. Because he did so, his death accomplished something eternal and glorious: it served as a substitute sacrifice for God's people, satisfying God's wrath against sin and achieving eternal salvation for all who repent and put their faith in him.

1. Skim through Matthew 27:32–61. What observations can you make about the humiliation and suffering Jesus Christ endured in the hours leading up to his death?

2. If it's true that the wages of sin is "death" (Rom. 6:23), why is it so important that Jesus actually, physically died in our place?

3. Why was the spiritual suffering of Jesus on the cross so much worse than the physical suffering (although that, too, was terrible)?

Resurrection

Review pages 131–32 in *Knowing God's Truth*

Jesus's physical resurrection from the dead meant that his sacrifice for sin on the cross was complete and acceptable to God. If Jesus's death on the cross had not fully covered and paid for the sins of God's people, he would have stayed dead; there would have been more debt for sin that had to be paid. But the very fact that Jesus did not stay dead proves that no more punishment exists for God's people; Jesus has truly paid the entire penalty for sin. When he rose bodily from the dead, he proved that he had conquered death—and would reign as the living Savior and Lord forever. Jesus's resurrection also gives us hope that all who belong to him by faith will one day rise again with eternal, glorified physical bodies like his.

1. Read 1 Corinthians 15:20–28. Why is Jesus Christ's physical resurrection such a fundamentally important reality for Christians? How does this doctrine give us hope for the future?

2. Why might it be dangerous to separate Jesus's death from his resurrection? What does the resurrection prove about what Jesus's death accomplished?

3. How does Jesus's physical, bodily resurrection give us hope for our eternal future, if we belong to him?

_____

_____

_____

JESUS'S *PRESENT REIGN*

Review pages 132–34 in *Knowing God's Truth*

After his resurrection, Jesus ascended into heaven and is currently seated and reigning at the right hand of God the Father. Jesus is physically present in heaven right now. From there, he mediates for God's redeemed people, serving as our intercessor before the holy God on the basis of his saving work in our place on the cross. Jesus rules over this world, sovereignly orchestrating all things for God's glory and the eternal good of his redeemed people. And Jesus is waiting for exactly the right moment to return in glory and power to judge the world and take his people home to the new heaven and new earth, where he will reign forever as the conquering King.

1. Read Hebrews 10:11–25. What are some of Jesus's present activities and concerns, according to these verses? Why are these activities of Jesus so encouraging for us as his redeemed people?

_____

_____

_____

2. While it is good to remember Jesus's humble suffering and crucifixion, why should we also intentionally remember where he is right now—and what he is currently doing?

_____

_____

_____

3. How should the present reign of Christ comfort us right now? Why is it good news to know that your faithful Savior is reigning over the world even when difficult things come into your life?

JESUS'S *FINAL JUDGMENT*

Review pages 134–36 in *Knowing God's Truth*

Jesus is going to return to this earth, and his second coming will not be secret and humble like his first coming, when he arrived as a baby in a manger. His return to earth will be dramatic, global, and powerful. When he comes back, Jesus will make himself known as the glorious God and the eternal Judge of all the earth. While we often think of God the Father as the great Judge (which is true), the Bible presents Jesus Christ himself as executing the judgment of God on all of his enemies at the last day. He is the gracious Savior, and he will accept all who turn to him in faith. But all who reject his offer of salvation will be eternally judged.

1. Read Revelation 19:11–21. How does this picture contrast with Jesus's suffering and humiliation on the cross?

2. Why is the concept of Jesus's return sometimes hard for us to grasp—and even difficult to believe?

3. How is the second coming of Jesus very good news for his people—and very bad news for those who have rejected him?

RESPONDING TO JESUS

Review pages 136–38 in *Knowing God's Truth*

In our study of theology, we always want to actively and intentionally connect our *heads* to our *hearts*. In other words, we want our learning *about* God to increase our love *for* God. So how should we respond to this Jesus we've been learning about? First, we should fear him, knowing that he is the risen Savior and the eternal Judge of the world. Second, we should worship him, giving him the glory and the praise that only he deserves. Third, we should love him, seeing him as the gracious Savior of sinners and the lover of our souls. Everything we've learned about Jesus should drive us toward greater admiration, love, worship, and service for him.

1. Read Revelation 5, noting especially the "new song" that is sung in praise of the Lamb. How should this heavenly scene guide our response to Jesus right now on earth?

2. How do you struggle to connect your "head" to your "heart" in your learning about God? What can make it so hard to do?

3. In what ways has this chapter increased your admiration for Jesus?

▼ SO WHAT?

As you conclude this chapter, jot down answers to the following application questions:

1. What are some ways you've been guilty of thinking less of Jesus than you ought? How has your study of Christology given you a bigger view of who he is?

2. How can understanding the person of Jesus Christ better help you understand your own salvation—and future eternal destiny—better?

THE DOCTRINE OF SALVATION

Now we turn to the very important doctrine of salvation. The technical title for this category of systematic theology is soteriology. Our plan in this chapter is to explain how the Old Testament anticipated God's great salvation through Jesus Christ, study the "order of salvation" as it is described in Scripture, and then think through very intentionally what happened on the cross and how God saves sinners through his Son, Jesus Christ. Hopefully by the end of this chapter, you will have a much better and broader understanding of the salvation that God offers to sinful people through the work of his Son.

As you begin, jot down answers to these initial questions:

1. When it comes to thinking about heaven and hell, why do many people today simply assume they're headed for heaven (if they think about it at all)?

2. Why is it so important for us to understand how God intends for human beings to be saved? Why might the question of how we are saved be the most important question for human beings to answer?

3. What questions do you have about God's salvation of sinners? What is confusing to you about the work of Jesus Christ in his death and resurrection?

THE EXCLUSIVITY OF CHRIST

Review pages 143–44 in *Knowing God's Truth*

Has someone ever tried to tell you that all religions are basically the same? This is a very common opinion today because the world has increasingly elevated the value of tolerance. Therefore, it seems likely that it will become more and more common for people to say, "It doesn't matter what religion you follow; they all say basically the same thing, and they all lead to some kind of salvation. The important thing is that we simply get along and coexist." The Bible's clear claim is quite different: eternal salvation comes through repentance and faith in Jesus Christ *alone*. This concept is often referred to as the "exclusivity of Christ"—the truth that sinful human people find eternal salvation exclusively through faith in Jesus—the Savior who died for sins and rose again from the dead.

1. Read Acts 4:12. What very clear point about the exclusivity of Christ do Peter and John make in this verse?

2. Why does the exclusivity of Christ offend many people today? How does it go against the grain of many people's opinions and preferences?

3. What is exclusive about God's salvation through Jesus? How is God's offer of salvation through Jesus also beautifully *inclusive*?

SALVATION AND THE OLD TESTAMENT

Review pages 145–48 in *Knowing God's Truth*

What we need to see from the Old Testament is that God's work in the lives of his ancient people built anticipation for the salvation—and the Savior—that would one day come. In the moments after the fall of Adam and Eve, God promised that Eve's "offspring" would one day crush the head of the serpent, Satan (Gen. 3:15). God's salvation of Noah and his family through the ark pointed forward to a greater rescue from judgment to come.

The sacrificial law, given through Moses, taught that human sin requires blood sacrifice. And the prophet Isaiah pointed God's people ahead toward a "suffering servant" who would be crushed in the place of God's people. The Old Testament anticipated—and pointed forward to—God's salvation through his Son.

1. Read Deuteronomy 18:15–22. How does Moses point forward to someone greater to come—and what does he say about this person?

2. Can you think of other Old Testament stories that gave a glimpse or a hint of what God's coming salvation through Jesus would look like?

3. Why is it helpful for us today (who live after the coming of Jesus) to still study and understand the Old Testament?

THE ORDER OF SALVATION
Election

Review pages 148–50 in *Knowing God's Truth*

In traditional Reformed theology, many scholars and theologians talk about the "order of salvation." This is a basic summary of how God works to save people. While some of the "steps" of salvation are difficult to distinguish from one another chronologically, the basic order in Reformed thought goes like this: election, regeneration, justification, sanctification, glorification. The first step, *election*, was the act of God to ordain whom he would save before time began. This truth reminds us that salvation is completely an act of God's power and grace. Salvation belongs to the Lord; all glory must go to him for saving sinners.

1. Read Ephesians 1:1–14. What does Paul make clear about God's election of his chosen people?

2. What is difficult to understand—or accept—in the verses you just read from Ephesians? Why might election be a difficult doctrine for many?

3. How does the doctrine of election remind us of God's primary role in our salvation? Why should this doctrine keep us humble?

Regeneration

Review pages 151–52 in *Knowing God's Truth*

The second step in the order of salvation is *regeneration*, which is also a powerful, gracious act of the God who is completely sovereign in our salvation. The word *regenerate* literally means "to bring to life." This doctrine reminds us, first, of the reality of our sin: we are spiritually dead, totally depraved, and absolutely unable to choose God by our own strength and volition. So if sinners are to be saved, God needs to act first; he must make dead sinners spiritually alive, by the power of the Holy Spirit, so that they can turn in repentance and faith to Jesus Christ. This is the doctrine of regeneration—and it comes even before repentance, faith, and justification in our order of salvation.

1. Read Ephesians 2:1–3. What does Paul make clear about the spiritual state of Christians *before* God acts to save them?

2. Read Ephesians 2:4–10. How does Paul remind his readers of God's work in their salvation—in spite of their spiritual deadness apart from Christ?

3. Why does the doctrine of regeneration (and the need for regeneration) follow naturally from the doctrine of total depravity, which we discussed earlier?

Justification

Review pages 152–54 in *Knowing God's Truth*

The next step in our order of salvation is *justification*. By God's grace—and the powerful working of the Holy Spirit in regeneration—sinners are enabled to come alive spiritually and then turn in repentance and faith to Jesus Christ as Savior and Lord. At this moment of faith, sinners are "justified" by God. The word *justification* carries a legal sense; God *declares sinners righteous* on the basis of Jesus's work in their place on the cross. God's justification of sinners doesn't happen because of anything they have done; this legal and just declaration of righteousness is because Christ—God's Son—has been perfectly righteous in their place, both in his perfect life of obedience and in his sacrificial, substitutionary death. All sinners who repent and place their faith in Jesus Christ are *justified* by his death and resurrection in their place.

1. Read Romans 4:1–8. How are we made right (declared righteous) before God, according to Paul?

2. Why is the doctrine of justification such good news for sinners who can never make themselves righteous before God through their own good works?

3. How does justification demonstrate that God is just, fair, and righteous?

Sanctification

Review pages 155–57 in *Knowing God's Truth*

In our order of salvation, the step that follows justification is sanctification. To be "sanctified" is to be made more and more holy—more like Jesus Christ—by the power and presence of the Holy Spirit, who indwells all who have placed their faith in Jesus. Specifically, we are talking here about what is called *progressive sanctification*, which takes place bit by bit, step by step, throughout the entire earthly life of every genuine Christian. Christians are active in this step of salvation in a way that they are *not* active in the other steps; as followers of Jesus Christ, indwelt by the Holy Spirit, we actively and joyfully participate in God's sanctifying work in us by seeking to obey God's word, put sin to death, and put on righteousness. Still, it is the power of the Holy Spirit that enables our spiritual growth as we strive to serve the Savior.

1. Read Ephesians 4:17–32. What are some of the evidences of sanctification that Paul seeks in the lives of genuine believers in Jesus Christ?

2. How are we active in our sanctification in a way that we are *not* active in our justification?

3. Why is it important for us to remember that our sanctification will never be fully completed in this life? Even so, why should genuine believers strive to be more and more sanctified?

Glorification

Review pages 157–59 in *Knowing God's Truth*

The final step in our order of salvation is *glorification*. This refers to our future hope that God's people one day will be made both physically and spiritually perfect—that is, glorified and made like Christ. When that time comes, Christians will be given new, perfect, immortal resurrection bodies. They will be physical bodies, but they will be perfected—incapable of growing sick or weary, or dying. Paul tells us that because Jesus has been resurrected in this way, we too will experience this kind of resurrection. In our new, glorified bodies, we will finally know what it is like to live in a world that is not infected with sin, in bodies that are not plagued by sin. When Jesus has made an end of sin, Satan, and death, we will finally know what this glorified and totally sanctified state of life is like!

1. Read 1 Corinthians 15:35–49. What hope does the Bible offer for Christians after they die? What is exciting to you in these verses?

2. What are some differences you will experience between life in your earthly body and life in your heavenly, glorified body?

3. Why is it such good news that we will one day be freed from even the presence of sin in our lives, hearts, and world?

ATONEMENT THEORIES

Review pages 159–62 in *Knowing God's Truth*

Jesus's death on the cross was a cosmically massive event, so many have sought to put forward ideas about what his death was really most centrally about. Scholars refer to these discussions as "atonement theories." The *Christus victor* theory of the atonement emphasizes Jesus's death as a victorious triumph over Satan, sin, and death. The *moral exemplar* theory of the atonement sees his death as an example of sacrifice that his disciples ought to follow. While these aspects of Jesus's death are true, traditional Reformed thought has insisted that *penal substitution* must be understood to be the central aspect of Jesus's death, meaning that the cross was the place where Jesus served as the substitute for God's sinful people, bearing the penalty for sin in their place.

1. Read Colossians 2:13–15. What particular result of Jesus's death does Paul emphasize in these verses?

2. Read Philippians 2:1–11. What particular application of Jesus's death does Paul make to his audience in these verses?

3. Why must we be careful never to lose the central idea of *penal substitution* when we think about the cross of Jesus Christ? What is lost when we forget this?

WHAT WAS ACCOMPLISHED AT THE CROSS?

Review pages 162–64 in *Knowing God's Truth*

When we ask what was accomplished at the cross, there are many ways to answer! Here are five words to help us understand how God acted to save sinners through the work of Jesus on the cross. *Reconciliation* refers to the way Jesus restored our relationship with God, which was broken through our sin. *Redemption* refers to the way Jesus's death bought us back for God, redeeming us from the curse and bondage of Satan, sin, and death. *Substitution/sacrifice* refers to the way Jesus truly offered himself in our place as the final sacrifice for our sins. *Propitiation* refers to the fact that Jesus bore the wrath of God against our sin on the cross so that his wrath was completely satisfied. Finally, *justification* refers to the fact that, by faith in Christ, God declares us righteous for all eternity. Praise God for his saving work!

1. Read Colossians 1:15–23. How is Paul showing us the beauty of God's salvation through Jesus Christ? What, specifically, is so beautiful?

2. Pick one of the five italicized terms above and write a couple of sentences about it. Why does this term demonstrate an encouraging truth for you?

3. What was new to you in the five words about Jesus's death on the cross?

▼ SO WHAT?

As you conclude this chapter, jot down answers to the following application questions:

1. What important lessons did you learn about your spiritual state—apart from Christ—in this chapter?

2. How did the truths about salvation in this chapter help you grow in your appreciation for God's gracious work in your life?

3. What ought to be our response to the God who has acted since before the beginning of time to save us through the work of his Son?

THE DOCTRINE OF HEAVEN AND HELL

The Bible is extremely clear that heaven and hell are very real places—not just theological ideas. It would be good for you to ponder your eternal future as you learn the concepts and lessons of this chapter. Also, as you become convinced of the reality of heaven and hell, you should be led to think more often about the need to share the gospel with others. Every human being that you know and see is bound for either hell or heaven. In this book, we have often noted the importance of accepting Jesus Christ as Savior and Lord. The human response to God's Son is what truly determines the eternal destiny of every human being. Hell is not an easy concept to talk about. In one sense, we should not be able to discuss it without sadness in our hearts as we think about people who have rejected God and his Son, Jesus Christ. Yet we will try to see how God's just and righteous character leads us to our belief in both hell and the glorious heavenly future to come.

As you get started, jot down some answers to these questions:

1. What are some common perceptions of heaven that you've heard from friends or acquaintances in your circle?

2. Why do many people today object to the idea of a literal, eternal hell?

3. What questions do *you* bring to this discussion about the doctrine of heaven and hell?

COMMON MISCONCEPTIONS

Review pages 171–73 in *Knowing God's Truth*

When people today think about heaven, they often picture a disembodied existence in a nonphysical place. But heaven (the one that is to come) will be a new heaven and new earth—a physical place for physically resurrected children of God to dwell with him forever. Life with God in the new heaven and new earth will be glorious, thrilling, and full of joy! When it comes to hell, many people imagine it as a place where Satan reigns. This is not true; hell is a place where God's just and righteous wrath is poured out on sin. Other people think about hell as a final destruction—but the Bible's teaching about hell presents it to us as a place of ongoing punishment without hope of a second chance.

1. Read Revelation 21:1–8. How might this passage help shape your understanding of both heaven and hell?

2. What other misconceptions have you heard about either heaven or hell?

3. Why is it good news that life in heaven for eternity will be physical, embodied life—not merely a spiritual existence? What does this teach us about God—and creation?

WHAT HEAVEN TEACHES US ABOUT GOD

Review pages 174–75 in *Knowing God's Truth*

The doctrine of God's aseity taught us that God does not need anything or anyone; he is perfectly holy, happy, and content in and of himself—and has been that way for all eternity. Yet the reality of the future of heaven for God's people teaches us about his heart of grace, generosity, and love toward his people. He invites us into an eternity of fellowship with him if we will trust his Son and believe his word. What a wonderful thing it is for us to know that, while God does not need us, he delights to share himself with us. It is God's desire to live with his people as their God—in the new heaven and new earth—for eternity to come!

1. Read 2 Thessalonians 1:5–12. What do these verses tell you about God's love and care for his people—those who are called "saints" of God through faith in Jesus?

2. Why would it be dangerous for us to suggest that God decided to create (and save) people because he was lonely or because he lacked something? What would that imply about God?

3. How should it encourage you to know that God does not need to offer you an eternal future with him—and yet he freely chooses to do this?

WHAT HELL TEACHES US ABOUT GOD

Review pages 176–77 in *Knowing God's Truth*

Hell exists, quite simply, because God is perfectly just, holy, and righteous. God will punish sin; in fact, he must punish sin in order to maintain the perfection of his just and righteous character. And all sin is an infinite offense against an infinitely holy God—by creatures whom he has made! Hell, then, shows us God's justice to punish sin. But even more than that, hell reminds us that God is angry at sin; he pours out his wrath against all unrighteousness and rebellion—every violation of his holy and perfect character. Hell also reminds us of what an eternal tragedy it is for anyone to reject the *one way* God has so graciously provided for sinners to be saved: repentance and faith in his Son, Jesus Christ, who died on the cross to bear the just wrath of God in the place of sinners.

1. Look at 2 Thessalonians 1:5–12 one more time. What do these verses tell us about those who oppose God and his Son, Jesus?

2. Why does the just, holy, and righteous character of God make the punishment of sin—and the existence of hell—necessary?

3. What does the doctrine of hell teach us about the seriousness of sin against the holy God?

_____

_____

_____

WHAT IS HEAVEN?

Review pages 177–79 in _Knowing God's Truth_

It's important to understand that when people talk about heaven, they can be talking about two different things, biblically speaking. Heaven right _now_ is a real place, where the risen Lord Jesus Christ is seated at the right hand of God the Father and the souls of dead believers in Jesus are present with him (even though their physical bodies have died, been buried, and decomposed). However, heaven in the _future_ will be a new thing: when Jesus returns, he will make all things new—and heaven and earth will come together. The physical bodies of believers in Jesus will be resurrected and reunited with their souls, and they will live forever with Jesus in the new heaven and new earth.

1. Read Luke 23:32–43. Note the conversation Jesus has with one of the criminals who is crucified alongside him—and the promise Jesus makes to him. What do we learn about heaven in this conversation?

_____

_____

_____

_____

2. How would you encourage someone whose believing mother has died? Where is her soul right now, according to the promise of the Bible?

_____

_____

_____

_____

3. What will be different—and better—about the new heaven and new earth that will one day come?

_____

_____

_____

_____

WHAT IS HELL?

Review pages 179–81 in *Knowing God's Truth*

Earlier, you considered some misconceptions about hell (many people are confused about this topic). It's important to remember that hell is not a place where God is absent—it's a place where his perfect, pure wrath against unrepentant sin is poured out for all eternity. This sounds frightening and horrifying—and it is. Hell is a place of God's perfect justice without the experience of his mercy and grace (which is offered to all who will repent and turn in faith to Jesus Christ). While we don't know exactly what this awful place will be like, the Bible uses images of fire to describe it, as well as pictures of agony and suffering. It's a somber topic to discuss—and the reality of hell should spur us on to share the life-giving gospel of Jesus Christ with those who don't yet believe.

1. Read Matthew 25:31–46. What does Jesus teach about eternal punishment—the reality of hell—in these verses?

_____

_____

_____

2. What is frightening to you about hell? How have you struggled to accept this doctrine or to understand its reality?

_____

3. How can the existence of hell motivate you to spread the gospel of Jesus Christ to those who do not yet believe in him?

COMMON QUESTIONS ABOUT HEAVEN

Review pages 181–84 in *Knowing God's Truth*

The Bible does not explain every aspect of our eternal life in the new heaven and new earth, leaving us with questions about what is ahead for us. *What will we do in heaven?* We can imagine that there will be joyful experiences for us—and even some form of good *work* that God has for us there. *Will people who are married in this life still be married in heaven?* No, human marriage will end (because human marriage is meant to point to the greater "marriage" between Jesus and his people, the church). *Will it be possible to sin in heaven?* No, we will no longer be able to sin! But the most beautiful and wonderful thing about heaven is that we will be with Jesus Christ, our Lord, under his perfect reign and in perfect fellowship with God, our Creator.

1. Read Matthew 22:23–33. What does Jesus clarify with regard to marriage in heaven? What else does Jesus say about our experience in heaven?

2. What are some other questions people might have about heaven that the Bible does not specifically answer?

3. Why is it so important that—in all of our thinking about what heaven will be like—we stay focused on the person of Jesus Christ?

COMMON QUESTIONS ABOUT HELL

Review pages 184–85 in *Knowing God's Truth*

The doctrine of hell also provokes many questions. *Will Satan rule hell for all eternity?* Contrary to what some think, Satan will not be in charge of hell (he will be finally judged by Jesus at his return). *Will the presence of earthly friends provide any comfort in hell?* Sadly, there will be no comfort from being in hell with other people, as they will all know the agony of God's punishment. *Will God be present in hell?* Hell will include the "presence" of God, but it will be manifested only in his terrible wrath against sin. Hell is the place where God's just wrath against sin is poured out. This is a sobering reality, and one that should humble us—and drive us to faith in Jesus Christ, whom God has put forward as the Savior for sinners.

1. Read Luke 16:19–31. What does Jesus teach us about hell through this parable?

2. Why do some people take the idea of hell so lightly today? Why is this so incredibly dangerous?

3. How can the doctrine of hell humble us? How can it remind us of the wonderful grace of God's salvation through Jesus Christist?

▼ SO WHAT?

As you conclude this chapter, jot down answers to the following application questions:

1. How does the study of the doctrine of heaven and hell teach us about the seriousness of sin—and the massive grace of our salvation through Jesus Christ?

2. What can you do in your life to embrace more of an eternal perspective every day? Why is it good to think regularly about the realities of heaven and hell?

3. The Bible reminds us often about the brevity of life—and the significance of eternity stretching out before us. How can these reminders shape our relationships with others? The way we invest our time? The way we use our words?

Chapter 9
THE DOCTRINE OF THE CHURCH

Hopefully, if you are a follower of Jesus Christ, you are involved in some kind of a local church community. As we discuss in this chapter, local churches have been the primary way in which the gospel of Jesus Christ has been taught, lived out, and passed on in the days since the resurrection and ascension of Jesus Christ. Although the church can often seem weak and imperfect, the Bible makes clear that it is God's main focus of work and witness in the world today. We are therefore learning about something that is very near to the heart of God. Our goal, as we begin this discussion, is to introduce you to the doctrine of the church. The formal name for this category of systematic theology is ecclesiology. It is important to note that this doctrine is especially applicable to you if you follow Jesus Christ, because church involvement should be at the very center of your spiritual life and your relationships with other believers in Jesus.

As you get going, jot down answers to the following questions:

1. How have you seen the local church to be a vital part of your life and growth in Jesus Christ?

2. What frustrations have you had with the local church? What criticisms of the church do you sometimes hear from people around you?

3. Why might it be dangerous to live a purely "personal" life of devotion to Jesus Christ without any significant engagement or relationships with God's people?

CHURCH BEGINNINGS

Review pages 193–95 in *Knowing God's Truth*

After Jesus's ascension into heaven, he sent his Holy Spirit to anoint the apostles (those who had been with him and learned from him) with special power to preach the gospel and to help many people follow him. Acts 2 records the first explosion of believers, as many people decided to put their faith in Jesus and become part of the early "church." The word *church* (*ecclesia* in Greek) simply means "gathering" or "assembly," so the early church was simply the *gathering* of followers of Jesus Christ. These gatherings began to be localized in certain towns as followers of Jesus organized and began meeting for worship, prayer, teaching, the Lord's Supper, and fellowship.

1. Read 1 Corinthians 1:1–3. What do you learn about the church from the way Paul describes the Corinthian believers? How does Paul think about these Christians?

2. Why was it so important for the first believers in Jesus Christ—during the first century—to begin gathering for worship in their towns and cities?

3. What type of leadership was needed as the church began to form and organize? Why are godly and well-qualified leaders important in a Christian community?

THE UNIVERSAL CHURCH

Review pages 195–97 in *Knowing God's Truth*

It's important to understand that there are really two ways to talk about "the church." We can speak of the *universal* church and the *local* church (sometimes also referred to as the *invisible* and the *visible* church). The universal (or invisible) church is made up of *all believers in Jesus Christ from all times and all places*. It is all of the people of

God who will share eternity together in the new heaven and new earth. Everyone who has repented and placed their faith in Jesus belongs to the universal church. One day, every believer in Jesus Christ will be gathered together to live with, worship, and serve the Lord Jesus Christ for eternity to come. On that day, the church will be complete and fully unified.

1. Read Revelation 7:9–17, John's vision of the universal church of Jesus Christ. What do you notice about this gathering of people?

2. What excites you about John's vision for the future gathering of God's diverse and global people? How should this help you think about the church in the world even now?

3. How should it impact your walk with God to know that you are part of the universal, invisible church of Jesus Christ—if you've put your faith in him?

THE LOCAL CHURCH

Review pages 198–200 in *Knowing God's Truth*

As we see what the Bible teaches about the local church, we can come to define it as *a localized manifestation of the universal church of Jesus Christ.* In other words, it is appropriate and biblically accurate to talk about local churches in the same category as the universal church. They are not different things; they are just localized "arms" of the universal church. The New Testament authors—the apostles—do not really have a category for a believer in Jesus Christ who is not living out his or her faith in the context of the local church in his or her town. In fact, it is impossible to obey much of the New Testament if we are not involved in local churches of Jesus Christ along with other believers. The assumption of the New Testament is that membership in the universal church of Jesus Christ (through faith) is lived out and practiced in the context of the local church.

1. Skim through Titus 1, noting some of Paul's instructions to this young pastor, who was overseeing young churches throughout Crete. What does Paul tell Titus to do?

2. What would you say are some of the most central and important activities of a healthy local church? Why?

3. Why is it important for a believer in Jesus Christ to be part of a local church, even though he or she already belongs to the universal church?

THE LORD'S SUPPER

Review pages 200–202 in *Knowing God's Truth*

The "sacraments" of the Lord's Supper and baptism are practices of the church that were instituted by Jesus in a very special way—unlike any other part of corporate worship. We can define a sacrament as a *physical sign of an invisible reality of God's Holy Spirit*. These practices are "holy"—that is, they are set apart as special ways in which the Holy Spirit promises to work in the lives of his people in the church. Because these are holy practices that Jesus instituted, he "attached" his presence to them in a special way. Thus, the sacraments are ways in which God communicates his grace to his people in the church. This is not his saving grace; baptism cannot save a person from sin! But God's gracious presence and blessing is given in a very real way to his people through the sacraments. The first of the sacraments, *the Lord's Supper*, is a spiritual meal—celebrated regularly by believers in the local church—through which we feed spiritually on Jesus, remember his body and blood given in our place to save us, and receive spiritual nourishment as we do so.

1. Read 1 Corinthians 11:23–34. What do you learn about the Lord's Supper in these verses? How does Paul make clear that this is a very serious meal?

2. Why is it so important for someone to understand clearly what the Lord's Supper means in order to partake of it rightly?

3. How has God used the Lord's Supper in your life (if you are a Christian and partake of it) to remind you of Jesus's death, call you to confession and repentance, and nourish your heart and soul?

BAPTISM

Review pages 203–5 in *Knowing God's Truth*

Baptism is the second sacrament that Jesus Christ instituted for his people in the local church. The picture of washing with water is a visible symbol and sign of the washing of sinners with the cleansing blood of Jesus, and of the working of the Holy Spirit, who "washes" over believers in Jesus in faith. Baptism is often referred to as the "new covenant sign" of the people of God; it "marks" God's people as belonging to him and being a part of his family, the church. Within the Reformed tradition, there are credobaptists, who believe that the sign of baptism should be administered only to those who have professed faith in Jesus Christ (and who should be fully immersed in water), and covenantal paedobaptists, who believe that the sign of baptism should be administered not only to professing Christians who are members of the visible church, but also to their children, who are part of the covenant family of God (the visible church) though they have not yet come to personal repentance and faith.

1. Read Matthew 28:16–20. How is baptism a central part of Jesus's great commissioning of his disciples to serve him in the world?

2. Do you come from a credobaptist or a covenantal paedobaptist church background? How have you heard the position to which you hold best argued and defended from Scripture?

3. Have you been baptized? If so, when? How has God used your baptism in your life? If you haven't been baptized, why not?

LEADERSHIP IN THE CHURCH

Review pages 205–7 in *Knowing God's Truth*

While there is certainly room for different "models" of church government within Christian churches that really love Jesus and believe the Bible, it seems that passages such as 1 Timothy 3, Titus 1, and others put forward a model of church government that is *elder-led* (specifically with a "plurality," or group, of elders). That is, the Bible seems to place a big emphasis on godly men who will serve as elders of local churches in order to lead the people of God well, teach them the gospel, exert spiritual discipline and authority, and guard against false teaching and behavior. Biblically, the role of pastor and elder seem to be the same, with deacons as a separate class of officers focused on the practical care of the members of the church and their needs. The qualifications for both elders and deacons are laid out in 1 Timothy 3 and Titus 1.

1. Read through (or skim over) 1 Timothy 3, which lays out clearly some qualifications for the officers of the church (elders and deacons). What do you notice about the moral and spiritual qualifications of these church leaders?

2. Why does it make sense for churches to have multiple elders leading and guiding the church? Why could a church led by just one person experience hardship and poor health?

3. What dangers might come if a church is led purely "democratically"—with the congregation voting on every decision rather than appointing elders who lead and establish oversight and direction for the church?

THE MARKS OF A TRUE CHURCH

Review pages 207–9 in *Knowing God's Truth*

In the Reformed tradition, the main three "marks" of the church are understood to be the preaching of God's word, the celebration of the sacraments (the Lord's Supper and baptism), and the exercise of church oversight and spiritual discipline. Biblically speaking, these seem to have been the fundamental building blocks of the local church from its earliest days in New Testament times. God's word was preached; the Lord's Supper and baptism were administered; and qualified men were set apart to serve, lead, and shepherd the church as elders and deacons. There are, of course, other regular activities that healthy local churches should be involved in—prayer, giving, acts of service, encouragement, evangelism, and many more—but the three key marks are to be characteristic of *every* true church.

1. Read 1 Timothy 4:11–16. What are some of the activities that should be going on in a healthy, biblically grounded local church, according to these verses?

2. Why should an entity that is *not* a local church not practice the sacraments—the Lord's Supper and baptism? Why is it so important that the sacraments be celebrated only in the context of a local church under the oversight of church leaders?

3. What marks of the church—and regular parts of worship—are most emphasized in your local church? Why do you think that is?

IMPLICATIONS OF THE DOCTRINE OF THE CHURCH

Review pages 210–12 in *Knowing God's Truth*

God loves the church! That is very clear in the pages of the New Testament (see Eph. 5:25–33). It's also clear that the New Testament apostles wrote their epistles with the assumption that believers in Jesus Christ would be actively involved in the local gathering of believers. The message of the New Testament is that involvement in the universal church (through faith in Jesus Christ) implies our involvement in the local church, where we live out our faith with other Christians. So the very practical conclusion to this discussion is that the local church is to have a central priority in the lives of followers of Jesus Christ around the world. The church, as the Bible makes clear, is to be the main center of spiritual formation, Bible teaching, fellowship, discipleship, and the celebration of the sacraments for believers in Jesus.

1. Read Titus 2, noting Paul's instructions to men and women in the church—of all ages. How should the generations be working together in the context of the local church, according to Paul?

2. What would you say to a Christian who says, "I love Jesus, but I have no need for the church"?

3. How does God's love for his church—with all her imperfections—point us again to his immense grace and mercy?

▼ SO WHAT?

As you conclude this chapter, jot down answers to the following application questions:

1. What was new to you as you considered the doctrine of the church in this chapter? What challenged you in terms of your own engagement in the local church?

2. How would you explain the connection between the local church and the universal church? Is everyone who is part of the local church part of the universal church? Why or why not?

3. Why should the sacraments—the Lord's Supper and baptism—be protected and taken seriously within the context of the church?

Chapter 10

THE DOCTRINE OF ANGELS AND DEMONS

In this chapter, you are going to dive into the systematic theology category of angels and demons—in other words, the spiritual realm. This topic fascinates some people; they obsess over angels and demons, and think often about their influence and impact in the world. Other people, though, never think about the reality of the spiritual realm; they function almost as if angels and demons do not even exist.

As you prepare to dive into these topics, jot down responses to these questions:

1. What might lead some people to be obsessed with the invisible spiritual realm? To what problems could such an obsession lead?

2. Why might some people almost never consider the spiritual realm and the existence of angels, demons, and Satan?

THE REALITY OF THE SPIRITUAL REALM

Review pages 215–17 in *Knowing God's Truth*

If you have not acknowledged before that angels and demons—and a complex spiritual realm—exist, then you need to do so now. The Bible is clear that angels are servants of God, who have acted (and still act) in God's world according to his will at various times and places. Demons, too, are mentioned in the Bible often; they are servants of Satan and oppose the work of God in this world. We also need to admit that there is real power in the spiritual world. While God is ultimately in control of all things, the power in the spiritual realm is greater than human power. We do not want to obsess over the involvement of angels and demons in this world, but we do want to examine carefully what Scripture teaches about the spiritual world and seek to apply right thinking and good biblical doctrine to our lives as we follow Jesus and come to understand reality in light of his good word. Finally, in all of our study and thinking about the spiritual world, we should return again and again to the lordship and rule of Jesus Christ—the only great King of the universe. He is declared to be the one who is over all rulers and authorities; in fact, he conquered Satan himself through his death and resurrection!

1. Why is it important to not minimize or dismiss the real power of Satan and his demonic servants?

2. How is the doctrine of creation important in our discussion of angels and demons? Why is that an important starting point?

3. What is encouraging about the eternal reign of Jesus Christ over all powers and authorities?

GOD AND THE SPIRITUAL REALM

Review pages 218–20 in *Knowing God's Truth*

Some people mistakenly believe that the world is in the midst of a "power struggle" between God and Satan. They think of God and Satan as two almost equal beings— God working for good, and Satan fighting against him for the advance of evil. This is a form of "dualism"—the belief that there are two equal forces in the universe (good and evil) that are in constant battle and tension with one another. But this is *not* the teaching of Scripture. The Bible, and particularly the doctrine of creation, reminds us that God is absolutely distinct from his creation—even the spiritual realm. Satan, as powerful as he is, is a created being; demons, too, were created by God. Long before angels and demons ever existed, the God of the Bible was reigning supreme and secure in himself. There is no power struggle going on; Satan can never hope to stand against God, although God has chosen to allow him to act in powerful ways for a time. God is absolutely sovereign over angels and demons—and Satan himself. God's people can rest secure in his final victory.

1. Read Genesis 1:1–2 and John 1:1–5. What do these passages tell us about God's role as Creator of all things—seen and unseen?

2. What is dualism? How is this idea unbiblical?

3. Why is it important to remember that, as powerful as Satan is, he is a creature who was made by God? How should this fact comfort us?

ANGELS
What Are Angels?

Review pages 220–22 in *Knowing God's Truth*

The Bible makes it clear that angels—unlike human beings—do not experience natural physical death like human beings because they are spiritual, nonmortal beings (they do not share in human institutions such as marriage, for example, and are not born physically as humans are). Angels were created by God to live forever; they do not grow old and die. While it seems that they can take on physical form, they are spiritual beings and are not human. It is clear from various encounters with angels by human beings in Scripture that they are incredibly glorious beings. While their glory does not even begin to compare with that of the God of the universe, it is noteworthy that the natural human response to these beings when they appear is first fear, then worship. God has granted incredible splendor and glory to angels.

1. Read Matthew 22:29–33. What does this passage help you understand about angels and their role? How do they function in relationship to God and to human beings?

2. Read Daniel 10:10–12. What should these verses help us remember about angelic beings—and specifically their role in service to God and the servants of God?

3. How should we rightly appreciate and respect angels? What must we *not do* with regard to angels that we *should do* with regard to God?

The Purpose of Angels

Review pages 222–24 in *Knowing God's Truth*

We see at least five God-given purposes for angels laid out for us in the pages of Scripture. First, they have a role in *announcing* the purposes and plans of God to his people—often making known a message from God or foretelling something he is about to do. Second, angels have a role of *protection*; God often uses them to guard his people in dangerous situations or shield them from their enemies. Third, angels set an example for humans in their constant *worship* of God. Fourth, God uses angels to *provide* for the needs of his people in some situations. Fifth, angels *serve* at the direction of God to accomplish his purposes in the world; we see this happening in various ways and at various times throughout the story of the Bible.

1. Read Luke 1:26–38. What would you say is the primary purpose and role of the angel in this account?

2. Why might God choose to accomplish some of his purposes (communication, protection, provision) through the service of angelic beings? What might he be teaching his people?

3. How does the existence of angels (and the knowledge that they serve God for the good of God's people) encourage you and make you praise and thank your God?

The Christian Response to Angels

Review pages 224–26 in *Knowing God's Truth*

As the angel commanded John, Christians should see angels as "fellow servants" of God with us (Rev. 22:9). We should recognize that since God made them for his purposes, actions, worship, and service, they stand alongside us in service and praise of him. This means, of course, that Christians are not to pray to angels or worship them in any way—no matter how glorious and powerful they may be. God alone is worthy of worship; prayer should be directed to him alone in the name of Jesus Christ alone. We will share heaven with these fellow servants of God, giving praise to the Creator of us all.

1. Read Revelation 22:6–9. How do these verses help correct a potentially flawed response to angelic beings?

2. Why might it be helpful for some Christians to think more about angelic beings?

3. What might be signs that one is obsessing about angels too much—and in a way that detracts from our exclusive worship of God?

DEMONS

What Are Demons?

Review pages 227–28 in *Knowing God's Truth*

It is extremely important to remember that demons, like angels, were created by God. Since nothing exists that God did not create, the logical conclusion is that demons were, at one point, made by God to be his good servants. Also like angels, demons are spiritual beings; they do not have physical bodies. They therefore do not live, grow old, and die like human beings, but exist in a spiritual state. Because of this, they have significant power and influence in the world, although not nearly to the extent of the almighty Creator God, who rules over them. The very essence of demons, according to Scripture, is evil to the core. While we do not know when their rebellion—their "fall" from heaven—actually occurred, Scripture is clear that demons are completely fallen, desperately evil, and in the service of the prince of demons—Satan himself.

1. Read James 2:18–19. What does James teach us about what the demons believe and fear?

2. Read 1 Timothy 4:1–3. What do we learn about demons in these verses?

3. Why should we respect the power of demonic beings who are under the control of Satan? Why must we not tremble at demons or be paralyzed by fear of them?

Who Is Satan?

Review pages 228–31 in *Knowing God's Truth*

The Bible does not give us a detailed account of Satan's rebellion against God and "fall from heaven." Jesus mentions it in Luke 10:18, but this verse does not go into much detail. We know that Satan was an angel of God, created by God to serve him. We know, also, that by the time Adam and Eve ate the forbidden fruit in the garden of Eden, Satan had fallen and was committed to opposing God and his people. Satan, then, is a powerful spiritual being who was created by God as an angel, but who infinitely and completely rebelled against God's rule. He is the most powerful of all demonic beings, although his power does not begin to compare to that of God. Satan rages against God and against God's people—and he will oppose God's plans until the day when he is finally defeated and judged by Jesus, and cast into the lake of fire.

1. Read Revelation 20:7–10. What do we learn in these verses about the final destiny of Satan?

2. What evidence do you see in the world today of the influence of Satan—the "ruler" of this world (John 16:11)?

3. What encouragement should you take from the picture in Revelation 20 of Satan's final judgment and defeat?

The Purpose of Demons

Review pages 231–33 in *Knowing God's Truth*

Satan is referred to in Scripture as the "father of lies" (John 8:44), and his servants, the demons, accompany him in creating deception on earth. Demons can, at times, "possess" people, although Scripture nowhere gives an example of a Christian being possessed by a demon. Additionally, demons carry out various attacks on God's people and God's purposes in this world. While we often don't know what evils and harms in our world can be directly attributed to demonic attack, we know that Satan and his servants hate Jesus and the gospel, so they will viciously oppose God's purposes until the return of Jesus Christ to earth.

1. Read Mark 5:1–20. What effect did demons have on the life of the man who was living amid the tombs? How did Jesus demonstrate his authority and power over these demons?

---

2. How might demonic deceptions and attacks manifest themselves in our world today? Read 1 Timothy 4:1–2. How might this passage help us see one way that demons can have influence in our world today?

---

3. How should the existence of demons affect the way you pray for God's protection and for his faithfulness to his purposes for his people?

The Christian Response to Demons

Review pages 233–35 in *Knowing God's Truth*

It is good for Christians to be on guard against the lies of Satan and his demons. Remember, deception is one of their primary functions; they delight to deceive people with words and teachings that are opposed to the life-giving gospel of Jesus Christ. When John calls believers to "test the spirits" (1 John 4:1), he is urging them to compare every teaching or impulse that emerges in the world against the truth of the gospel—that Jesus Christ is the Son of God sent to be the Savior of all who believe. We should remember that demons are constantly pursuing the deception and destruction of people by turning them away from Jesus, so we should be watchful. But we should always remain confident in the power of Jesus Christ and of the Holy Spirit, who indwells us by faith in Jesus. The one who is in us is greater than the one who is in the world.

1. Read 1 John 4:1–6. How should believers evaluate the influence of demonic deception on earth, according to these verses? What are some "tests" that Christians can apply to various teachings or philosophies?

2. What might it look like to be more on our guard against the deceptive and destructive impact of demons in our world?

3. Why must we never fear demons? How can the final judgment of Jesus Christ give us comfort and hope?

▼ SO WHAT?

As you conclude this chapter, jot down answers to the following application questions:

1. How has reading this chapter and becoming more biblically informed about both angels and demons affected your life?

2. How can the existence, roles, and purposes of angels and demons increase your love, worship, and trust in your God and Savior?

Chapter 11

THE DOCTRINE OF LAST THINGS

Our topic of study for this chapter in systematic theology is eschatology, which means "the study of the end times." Obviously, this chapter will take us mainly into the biblical book of Revelation, which is the primary place where we see the Bible's teaching about this doctrine. As you may know, there are many different viewpoints on the exact timing and meaning of the events that Revelation depicts, as well as on the symbolism and metaphors that this apocalyptic book uses. Our goal in this chapter is to lead you to some clarity regarding these different viewpoints so that you can begin studying Scripture on your own and come to your own conclusions.

As you begin, jot down answers to these initial questions:

1. When you think about the end of the world, what do you picture? What sources (books, movies, sermons, etc.) have most influenced your view of the end times and the end of the world?

2. Why is it important for Christians to understand what the Bible teaches about the last things—the return of Jesus and the end of this world?

3. Where might some Christians disagree about what exactly the end of the world will be like? What are some big points and truths about which all true Christians should agree?

BEGINNING PRINCIPLES FOR ESCHATOLOGY

Review pages 239–41 in *Knowing God's Truth*

There are different perspectives on the end times, so there are points about which faithful, Bible-believing Christians sometimes need to "agree to disagree." However, there are some foundational biblical truths about the last things that all Christians believe. Biblical Christians believe that Jesus Christ will really physically return in glory to judge the world. They believe that there will really be a final physical resurrection and judgment of every human being. All Christians believe that God will really establish a new heaven and new earth, where his redeemed people will dwell with him—and that unbelievers will face punishment in hell for all eternity. True believers trust that Satan will really be finally conquered and judged, and sin will be no more. We want to cling to these core biblical truths even as we work toward our own conclusions about the specifics of eschatology.

1. Read Revelation 21:22–27. What is pictured in these verses? What do these verses clearly predict about what will happen at the end of the world?

2. What questions do you bring to the table with regard to the study of last things?

3. Why might some people dismiss this area of doctrine as a waste of time? Why *should* Christians carefully search the Scriptures to see what God's word teaches about the end of our world?

APOCALYPTIC LITERATURE

Review pages 241–43 in *Knowing God's Truth*

When we study eschatology, we generally delve into the "apocalyptic" literary genre of Scripture, which includes the book of Revelation, and parts of Daniel and other books. It's important to know some key aspects of apocalyptic literature in the Bible. First, this kind of literature contains graphic images. Jesus, for example, is pictured in Revelation in ways that would look strange if we took every description literally; the language is telling us what he is like, not giving literal physical descriptions. Also, apocalyptic literature describes cosmic drama. In other words, when you step into apocalyptic literature, you are going to be dealing with issues that pertain to all of humanity and all of creation. These issues include judgment, the return of Christ, the defeat of Satan, and the eternal reign of the followers of Jesus. Finally, apocalyptic literature often has a future focus. Yet apocalyptic literature, broadly, is about the "revealing" of the hidden and mysterious purposes of God—in the past and present, as well as the future.

1. Read Revelation 12:1–6. What is unfamiliar and confusing in this passage? How is it clear that this passage is part of a distinct genre of Scripture—unlike Paul's letters or the Gospels, for example?

2. Why is it so important for us to distinguish between the different literary genres of the Bible? How might we read, study, and apply different genres in slightly different ways?

3. What would you say is the chief purpose of apocalyptic literature in the Bible?

KEY TERMS OF ESCHATOLOGY

Review pages 244–46 in *Knowing God's Truth*

Before we dig into the various views on eschatology, it will be helpful to introduce several key terms that come up often in discussions of this category of theology. The *tribulation* generally refers to the time of trouble, persecution, violence, and suffering that is presented in Scripture as directly preceding the return of Jesus Christ and the final judgment of the world. While the Bible certainly points to this concept, it is not absolutely clear about how we should understand it. Many premillennialists understand the tribulation to be a literal seven-year period, near the very end of the world, that will either begin or end with the rapture of believers in Jesus to heaven. Amillennialists take the tribulation to be a symbolic way of talking about the general suffering and violence that began in the world after Christ's ascension and will continue until his return. Finally, most postmillennialists believe that the great tribulation has already happened—at some point during the first century. The concept of the *rapture* has to do with the "taking up" of believers to be with Jesus. While all biblical Christians believe that Christ will one day take them to be with him forever in the new heaven and new earth, there are different opinions as to how and when—and in what stages—this will actually happen. The *millennium* refers to the one thousand-year reign of Christ on earth, which is described especially in Revelation 20. There are varying interpretations with regard to whether or not this should be taken to be a literal or a figurative reign of Christ on earth, whether or not the thousand years is a literal time period or a symbol of fullness, and even whether or not Christ will return before or after this millennium. The *antichrist* is understood to be a great deceiver who will have power in the world before Christ's return—although the identity of this antichrist is very debated among Christians.

1. Skim through Matthew 24 (sometimes called Jesus's "Olivet Discourse"), in which Jesus points ahead to the last days. What questions does this passage raise? What are some clear truths that emerge from this passage?

2. What terms related to eschatology are new to you?

3. What remaining questions do you have about the Bible's teaching about the last days?

PERSPECTIVES ON ESCHATOLOGY
Dispensational Premillennialism

Review pages 247–48 in *Knowing God's Truth*

In general, the different perspectives on eschatology are separated by the way they understand the millennium. The millennium, which is mentioned in Revelation 20, is the label that has been given to the one thousand-year reign of Christ on earth. There are four main perspectives/viewpoints on how this millennium relates to our understanding of the final days of this earth. The first perspective, called dispensational premillennialism, holds to a very literal view of much of what is taught in Revelation and other apocalyptic passages in the Bible. People from this perspective see the thousand-year reign of Christ as being a thousand literal years on earth rather than a symbol of a "fullness" of time. They also look at Revelation 7 and see the group of 144,000 people from Israel there as a literal group of ethnic Jews who turn to Christ rather than as a picture of the fullness of true and spiritual Israel (all believers in Jesus Christ). Dispensational premillennialism also holds, based on Revelation 20, that Jesus Christ's return to earth will come before ("*pre*") the millennium. Therefore, people from this perspective believe that the Bible teaches that Jesus will return to earth and reign with some of the believers on earth for a literal thousand-year period, then the final battle against Satan will happen and the final judgment will come. Dispensational premillennialists and historic premillennialists agree generally on this point about the timing of Jesus's return (before his reign on earth). Most dispensational premillennialists, though, believe in a secret rapture of believers that will occur before the tribulation, the seven-year period of trial, trouble, and persecution that is described in Revelation and in Matthew 24.

1. Read Revelation 20:1–6. What are some ways in which people could interpret the events being described in these verses (in terms of their meaning, timing, etc.)?

2. Why should there be room for some disagreement among Christians about the timing and meaning of some of the events described in the book of Revelation?

3. What strengths do you see in the dispensational premillennialist perspective to the end times? What weaknesses do you see?

Historic Premillennialism

Review pages 249–51 in *Knowing God's Truth*

While historic premillennialists take much of Revelation in a "futurist" way, they are not as tightly literal in their interpretation as dispensational premillennialists, in general. Many historic premillennialists, for example, are comfortable thinking about the millennial reign of Christ as not a literal thousand-year reign, but as a reign for a fullness of time. They can see the number one thousand as symbolic of fullness, which would be very consistent with the way numbers are used in apocalyptic writings elsewhere. Historic premillennialists hold that, in accordance with a literal interpretation of Revelation 20, Christ will return to earth before his millennial reign on earth with believers. They look for a great return of Christ to earth, a period of time when he will reign visibly on earth with great power, and then a final judgment before his great throne of all people who have ever lived. Historic premillennialism differs from dispensational premillennialism, though, in the timing of the rapture of believers in relation to the great tribulation. Historical premillennialists hold that, according to Revelation 7:14 (and other places in Scripture), it seems that believers in Jesus Christ will be present for at least some of the tribulation and will have to endure it by faith in Jesus Christ. They reject the notion of a secret rapture and see more of a continuity (compared to the dispensational premillennial perspective) between Old Testament Israel and the new covenant people of God—the church.

1. Read Revelation 7:9–17. What great hope do you see in this passage? What seems to be pictured in this wonderful scene?

2. What strengths do you see in the historic premillennialist perspective on the last days?

3. What weaknesses do you see in this perspective?

Amillennialism

Review pages 251–53 in *Knowing God's Truth*

The general approach of amillennialism (which means "no millennium") is to see the apocalyptic genre of Scripture as working in an essentially *nonliteral* way. For those who hold to this viewpoint, numbers, events, and even individuals that are presented by the book of Revelation should often be taken to represent *spiritual realities*, but not necessarily tangible people or real events. This approach to the biblical text comes out, for example, in the amillennial view on the millennium. Amillennialists do not read Revelation 20 as predicting things that will happen in the future, with Christ returning to earth and literally reigning here for a time. Rather, they see the millennium as a figurative picture of what is happening right now as Christ reigns over the earth from the right hand of God as the risen Lord and Savior. They regard the binding of Satan that is described in Revelation 20 as a metaphorical holding back (to some extent) of Satan's influence in the world through the death and resurrection of Christ, allowing the gospel to grow and flourish in the world. This perspective sees much of what is described in Revelation as having already happened (or as happening now in the spiritual realm during the age of the church), although it still holds to a literal, physical return of Christ to judge the world and create a new heaven and earth for his resurrected people.

1. Skim through Revelation 20—the entire chapter. Consider again some of the different ways this chapter could be interpreted (in timing, meaning of words/events, etc.). Jot down some observations and questions.

2. What are some strengths of the amillennial position?

3. What might be some weaknesses?

Postmillennialism

Review pages 254–55 in *Knowing God's Truth*

While postmillennialists agree with premillennialists that much of Revelation is to be taken as speaking of real events, real people, and real places, they see many of these events as having taken place in the past—in the years following Jesus's ascension to heaven. The antichrist, then, is seen as Nero or one of the other Roman emperors who brutalized the Jews and persecuted God's people. The tribulation is understood as a great time of suffering during the first century. Postmillennialists also disagree with amillennialists by affirming that the millennium is a real visible reign of Christ on earth that is still to come. Postmillennialists (at least some of them) have a very real hope that the millennial reign of Christ has already begun; in that case, things on earth will gradually get better and better (or more influenced by the gospel and the church) as more and more people follow Jesus and he begins to rule more visibly and powerfully in this world until he ultimately returns in power to judge, raise the dead, and reign forever.

1. Read Ephesians 2:1–7. How do these verses point to the way believers are "raised" with Christ to reign with him? Why do these verses offer great hope?

2. What are some strengths of the postmillennialist position?

3. What might be some weaknesses of this interpretive approach?

APPLICATIONS OF ESCHATOLOGY

Review pages 258–60 in *Knowing God's Truth*

Hopefully you've been convinced about the importance of studying eschatology. This category of systematic theology should lead people toward a real and vibrant personal obedience to Jesus, as well as love for him. The knowledge of the last things and a vision of the end of the world should make his people want to follow him carefully and listen to his words. So even though eschatology deals with cosmic and global themes, it should always have a very practical application in our lives. Discussions about the final days of this earth and the coming judgment of Jesus should always make us consider carefully how we are living (or not living) for Jesus right now. Also, John concludes his introduction to the book of Revelation by saying, quite simply, that the time is "near" (1:3). This should lead to an important application for our lives as Christians—one that Jesus points to clearly in all that he says in Matthew 24: we must be ready. Jesus pictures it as staying "awake"—anticipating his return to earth and being constantly watchful. This does not mean, of course, that we stop being responsible or taking care of various parts of our lives. But it does mean that we think often about the return of Jesus and let the reality of the coming day impact our perspective, our words, and our actions toward others.

1. Read Revelation 1:1–3. How does John's introduction to the book of Revelation (which records his visions of God's work in the world—past, present, and future) help and guide us in our approach to studying eschatology?

2. What are some *practical* applications of the realities of the last days? How should the coming return and judgment of Jesus make a difference in your life right now?

3. How can you be *ready* and *awake* as you wait for Jesus's return?

▼ SO WHAT?

As you conclude this chapter, jot down answers to the following application questions:

1. What is the biggest change in your life—right now—that you should make in light of Jesus's impending return to earth as Judge, Savior, and King? How should your thoughts, words, and actions change in light of this future reality?

2. How have you been more convinced that Christians should work hard to understand eschatology? How might you study—and come to your own convictions about—all that the Bible teaches in this area?

Chapter 12

THE DOCTRINE OF THE HOLY SPIRIT

In this final chapter, you are going to learn more about the Holy Spirit—the third person of the Trinity. If you are like most Christians, you probably do not think very often—or very clearly—about the work of the Spirit. You probably know much more about God the Father and God the Son (Jesus) than you do about God the Holy Spirit. In this chapter, then, our goal is to examine all that the Bible has to teach us about the third person of the Trinity, whom we worship as one God in three persons—the Father, the Son, and the Holy Spirit.

As you get going, jot down answers to these initial questions:

1. Why might many Christians think less often about God the Holy Spirit than about God the Father and God the Son? What questions do you think people in your circles have about the Holy Spirit?

2. What points of confusion or questions have you had as you've thought about the Holy Spirit?

THINKING ABOUT THE HOLY SPIRIT

Review pages 265–66 in *Knowing God's Truth*

Some churches hardly ever mention the Holy Spirit. In fact, many Christians go through life rarely ever thinking—or talking—about the Spirit. This has led some people to call God's church to a return to a focus on the Holy Spirit because he has been so "forgotten." In one sense, this is good and right; Christians do need to remember that the God who reveals himself to us in Scripture is one God in three persons, and each person of the Trinity is distinct and fully God in himself. Yet the Holy Spirit nowhere demands a sole focus on himself. His role actually has to do with enabling the worship of the Father and the Son. Other Christians today are very focused on the work of the Spirit. His work is a focal point in their churches, and they ask the Holy Spirit to reveal himself and work in powerful ways in the lives of Christians. While it is good that such churches are so concerned with seeing God work and move actively today, the danger here is that the work of the Holy Spirit can be confused. Sometimes, a focus on spiritual gifts and new "prophecies" that are attributed to the Holy Spirit can take a wrongly central place in church life.

1. Read John 16:13–15. What are some of the actions of the Holy Spirit that Jesus describes in these verses? How might thinking about these actions help us begin to discover some of the main purposes of the Spirit?

2. Why is it important to understand the specific role and work of the Holy Spirit—especially in relation to the roles and works of the Father and the Son?

3. How have you seen an underemphasis on the Holy Spirit? What might an overemphasis (or misguided emphasis) on the work of the Spirit look like?

THE IDENTITY OF THE HOLY SPIRIT

Review pages 267–69 in *Knowing God's Truth*

We need to affirm from Scripture that the Holy Spirit is the third person of the Trinity, who is revealed to us as one God in three persons. Each of these persons is fully God in himself; these persons are distinct, and yet God is ultimately one. This is a mystery that we need to acknowledge, for we do not fully grasp or understand it. However, there is no doubt that the Holy Spirit is fully God. In many places in the New Testament (such as the introduction to 1 Peter), the Holy Spirit is named with the Father and the Son as God. So while the term *Trinity* is never actually used in the Bible, the concept is certainly there. Jesus—God the Son—at one point took on a human and physical body. He now lives and reigns in a resurrected and glorified body; he will keep that body forever and will reign in this visible and physical way over his people in the new heaven and new earth. The Holy Spirit, unlike Jesus, does not have a physical body. It is best to understand him as a spirit—invisible, and yet with all the power and identity of God himself. To go much further down this road, in terms of the essence of the Holy Spirit, is to say more than what the Bible tells us.

1. Read Genesis 1:26–27. What does the plural language ("Let *us* . . .") imply about the role of the three persons of the Trinity in creation? Why is this an important point to remember as we begin to consider God the Holy Spirit?

2. Why is it important to talk about the Holy Spirit in connection with the other two persons of the Trinity—the Father and the Son?

3. What are some ways in which God the Holy Spirit is clearly distinct from God the Son (Jesus)?

THE HOLY SPIRIT'S ROLES

Regeneration

Review pages 269–71 in *Knowing God's Truth*

"Regeneration" refers to the miraculous work of God to make sinners "come alive," repent of sin, and trust Christ as Savior and Lord. We know, from Ephesians 2:1–3, that apart from Christ, all human beings are not just bad; they are actually "dead" in sins (v. 1) and servants of Satan (v. 2). Romans 1–2 makes clear that all people are under God's wrath because of sin and unrighteousness. Biblical passages such as these lead us to the doctrine of total depravity, which means (among other things) that sinful human beings can never actually decide to trust God by their own power and strength. So there needs to be a miraculous work of God on the human heart. He has to "regenerate" sinners' hearts and enable them to turn to him in faith. This act of regeneration is pictured as coming from the Holy Spirit of God.

1. Read John 3:1–21. What did Jesus imply about what needed to happen in Nicodemus's life and heart? How did he point to the work of the Spirit in causing a person to be "born again"?

2. How does the doctrine of regeneration flow naturally from a right understanding of human sin and depravity?

3. Why is the Holy Spirit's active role in regeneration such good news for dead and helpless sinners?

Sanctification

Review pages 272–73 in *Knowing God's Truth*

The Bible makes clear that the Holy Spirit has a unique and distinct role in Christians' sanctification—the lifelong process of becoming more like Jesus and growing in holiness. This truth emerges from several basic teachings of the Bible. First, through faith in Jesus, the Holy Spirit indwells individual believers. The New Testament teaches that Christians are temples—dwelling places—for God's Holy Spirit (1 Cor. 6:19). The Spirit literally dwells within Christians by faith. Second, the Spirit also leads believers. This is Paul's teaching in Romans 8:14. Those who are apart from Christ are led by the flesh; they are slaves to sin. But Christians, who trust and follow Christ Jesus as Savior and Lord, are led by the Spirit, who dwells in them. The Spirit helps instruct them in God's word and helps them say no to sin. Finally, the Spirit helps Christians in prayer. In Romans 8:26, Paul talks about the Holy Spirit helping Christians pray to God—even when they do not know what to pray. This same Spirit, according to Paul, reminds Christians that they really do belong to God, and aids and empowers them in every aspect of their walk with Christ and obedience to God's word.

1. Read Romans 8:1–17. Where does the power for holiness, described by Paul, ultimately come from?

2. How does the Holy Spirit play an integral role in the sanctification of believers in Jesus Christ?

3. Why is it not possible for a sinful person to become more holy and obedient simply by his or her own strength?

Worship

Review pages 274–76 in *Knowing God's Truth*

God the Holy Spirit, who inspired the words of Scripture as they were spoken and written down by human servants of God, continues to work through the inspired, written word of God in the lives of God's people today. By this means, he convicts, rebukes, confronts, and turns hearts toward repentance from sin and toward faith in Jesus Christ. We must remember that in this work, the Holy Spirit aims to glorify Jesus. He never works to bring glory to himself as a distinct person of the Trinity. Rather, he seeks to illuminate God's word and lift up Jesus to people as beautiful, glorious, powerful, and gracious. So when we worship Jesus Christ as Savior and Lord, we are honoring the Holy Spirit; this is what he wants us—and helps us—to do!

1. Read 2 Peter 1:16–21. What role did the Holy Spirit play in God's gift of the "prophetic word" to his people?

2. Why is it important to connect the work of the Holy Spirit to the word of God?

3. How is the work of the Spirit tied to the worship of the Son? Why is the Spirit honored when we sing praises to Jesus?

THE HOLY SPIRIT AND SPIRITUAL GIFTS
Spiritual Gifts in the Early Church

Review pages 276–78 in *Knowing God's Truth*

There is no doubt that what happened in Acts 2 was the direct result of the working of the Holy Spirit. In fact, Jesus had promised his disciples that this would happen; he had told them that after they waited awhile in Jerusalem, the Holy Spirit would descend on them in power and they would proclaim the gospel from Jerusalem to all nations. The specific purpose of tongues in that original context seems to have been to facilitate the initial gospel explosion that started at Pentecost. Near the end of Acts 2, we learn that about three thousand people put their faith in Jesus Christ after Peter's first great sermon about the Savior. As the church grew and spread, miraculous signs (gifts of the Holy Spirit) sometimes accompanied the preaching of the gospel. But even though these signs were prevalent in those early days, there is no indication anywhere in Scripture that the miraculous gifts of the Holy Spirit were intended to be "normative" (normal or regular) for *every* believer who would ever follow Jesus Christ.

1. Read Acts 2:1–41 (or at least skim through it). What powerful signs accompanied the coming of the Holy Spirit at Pentecost?

2. In Acts 2, what specific purpose did the apostles' speaking in tongues accomplish? What was the result for people who heard the gospel preached in their own languages?

3. Why is it important to understand that the miraculous gift of tongues is nowhere in Scripture promised for every believer in Jesus Christ?

Spiritual Gifts in the Church Today

Review pages 278–80 in *Knowing God's Truth*

As we think about spiritual gifts in the church today (and especially the so-called "sign gifts" of the Spirit), we must be very careful not to limit God by saying that he "cannot" or "will not" work in a certain way. However, we also should not see tongues (or other miraculous gifts) as normal parts of the Christian life or as aspects that are to be expected or required from Christians who are really "filled" with the Holy Spirit. Such thinking is dangerous and unbiblical, so it must be rejected. There are entire groups of people—even denominations— that insist there is a "second baptism of the Holy Spirit," separate from conversion, that people should expect and pray for. This "filling," they think, is accompanied by signs such as speaking in tongues. The Bible nowhere teaches that something like this is normal or required for believers. The only filling of the Holy Spirit for Christians—and the only filling that they need—happens at conversion, when Christians are indwelt by the Holy Spirit through faith in Jesus Christ. Christians who do believe that the gift of tongues, in particular, is still applicable today should follow the careful instructions of the apostle Paul in 1 Corinthians 14. Finally, no matter what one believes about the applicability of spiritual gifts today, the main focus for every Christian should not be on gifts but on the gospel of Jesus Christ. That was Paul's focus; it was why he could say that he would rather speak just a few intelligible words about Jesus than many in tongues if no one could understand them (1 Cor. 14:19).

1. Read 1 Corinthians 14. What are some of Paul's instructions for how—and when— speaking in tongues should be a part of church life? What does Paul say is *better* than speaking in tongues?

2. Why is it dangerous for churches to place the gift of speaking in tongues on a pedestal—overemphasizing it and urging Christians to pursue it?

3. What are some other spiritual gifts that are celebrated in the New Testament? How might the church honor and use those gifts?

THE CHRISTIAN RESPONSE TO THE HOLY SPIRIT

Review pages 281–82 in *Knowing God's Truth*

So how does a follower of God honor the Holy Spirit? First, we remember that our glorious God and Savior has existed eternally as one God in three persons: the Father, the Son, and the Holy Spirit. When we think about God, we should consider the Trinity—our marvelous, mysterious, all-powerful, three-person God! Second, we should honor the Holy Spirit by studying and listening to God's word, which the Spirit inspired. We honor the Holy Spirit by taking these inspired words seriously and living according to them. Third, we honor the Holy Spirit by glorifying Jesus. The Spirit is delighted when the Son is lifted up in praise by God's people. Finally, we honor the Holy Spirit by pursuing sanctification—cooperating with his powerful work within us to enable us to put sin to death and put on righteousness as we obey our God more and more.

1. Read Romans 6:1–14. How should the Spirit play a role in our daily walk with God—our fight against sin and our obedience to God's word?

2. What are some ways in which it is evident that the Holy Spirit is living and active in your life and heart?

3. How can you obediently cooperate with the Holy Spirit as a follower of Jesus Christ?

▼ SO WHAT?

As you conclude this chapter, jot down answers to the following application questions:

1. What did you learn about God the Holy Spirit in this chapter that was new to you or that you had not considered deeply before?

2. How will you seek to honor God the Holy Spirit in your life right now? What adjustments might you need to make in the way you think about the Holy Spirit?

3. What remaining questions do you have about the Holy Spirit that you could discuss with a parent, a pastor, or a teacher?

More *Knowing God's Truth* Resources

In his book, **Knowing God's Truth**, Jon Nielson provides a clear, meaningful, and practical approach to the basics of systematic theology, including Scripture, man, sin, church, and more.

In the **Knowing God's Truth Video Study**, Nielson uses 10—12 minute videos to explore each chapter of the book, summarize the main points, and give biblical application. Ideally used alongside the companion book and workbook, this study is great for both small groups and individuals.

For more information, visit **crossway.org**.